Magickal Ric

Occult Rituals for Manifesting Money

Damon Brand

THE GALLERY OF
MAGICK

Copyright © 2015 Damon Brand

All Rights Reserved. This book may not be reproduced, in whole or in part, in any form or by any means electronic or mechanical, including photocopying, recording, or by any information storage retrieval system now known or hereafter invented, without written permission from the publisher, Damon Brand.

Disclaimer: Consider all information in this book to be speculation and not professional advice, to be used at your own risk. Damon Brand is not responsible for the consequences of your actions. Success depends on the integrity of your workings, the initial conditions of your life and your natural abilities so results will vary. The information is provided on the understanding that you will use it in accordance with the laws of your country.

CONTENTS

What This Book Can Do
How to Make Money with Magick
Money and Pleasure
Enjoying Money Magick
The Splendor of Money
The Balance of Money
Taking the Money Out of Magick
Making the Magick Safe
Emotional Alchemy
How Your Money Will Manifest
The Act of Magick
The Master Money Ritual
Discover Your Secret Source of Money
Ritual to Increase Sales
Ritual for Buying and Selling
Get Somebody to Pay Up
The Genius Rituals
Attract Money Through Perception
Chance Money Attraction
The Gambling Ritual
Unleashing the Flow of Money
Getting Money to Flow
When The Magick Works
Pronunciation Guide

What This Book Can Do

This book reveals the most treasured secrets of money magick, developed from ancient knowledge and modern occult technology. The work has been crafted by The Gallery of Magick during the past thirty years. The major workings in this book have never been published before, in any form.

Where the *Magickal Cashbook* gave just one method for attracting a small burst of money, and *Wealth Magick* worked on long-term career enhancement, this book contains practical rituals that continually manifest money. You can use them as needed, one at a time, or use them all at once if you need to get money flowing.

Magick can help you to grow spiritually, but unless you actually perform rituals to make valuable changes in the real world, you haven't begun to touch the true potential of magick. Creating money with magick is one of the most direct and exciting ways to experience the raw power of the occult.

This proven magick works safely, without wands, herbs, incense or candles. There is no need to pay the spirits, and there is no karma or spiritual backlash. You get what you deserve, you get it fast and you get to spend it any way you want.

The main rituals include The Master Money Ritual, which is designed to increase the overall flow of money in your life using a sigil that contains a secret pattern of magickal symbols.

You are also shown how to discover your Secret Source of Money, which can provide new streams of unexpected income. There is a Ritual To Increase Sales, for anybody who sells a product of any kind, and a Ritual For Buying and Selling that ensures that you get the best deal when you are buying or selling anything, from a small item to a house or business. When you are owed money, there's a ritual to Get Somebody to Pay Up.

In the second part of the book I cover The Genius Rituals. These rituals employ a set of unique sigils to call on intelligent and helpful spirits.

The first genius ritual shows you how to Attract Money Through Perception, which is ideal for anybody who deals or trades in any way, especially if you work with the stock market. This ritual is also ideal when you are trying to find the best course of action to take in a money-making situation.

The Chance Money Attraction ritual employs the power of Nitika (who was called on in my popular *Magickal Cashbook*) in harmony with several other genius spirits, to bring money out of the blue.

The final genius ritual is used to enhance your chances of success when gambling.

There is also a technique for adding extra energy to your magickal workings. This energy creation technique can be used to empower all the rituals in this book, and any other magick you perform, making it one of the most potent sections of this volume.

The book closes with a look at methods for opening the magickal flow of money.

Riches come in many forms. This book encourages a continual flow of money from unexpected sources, as well as improving your financial luck in several key areas.

If you are completely new to magick, know that this magick is safe and effective, and will work whether you believe in it or not. Work with the rituals as instructed, suspend your disbelief, see the results and discover a new way of interacting with reality. If you are an experienced occultist, I've ensured that the book is packed with previously unpublished material and methods, so that even the most proficient magickal workers will discover something new.

I cannot promise a lottery jackpot or a sudden change that will make you instantly rich, but this magick can help riches to flow through your life. If you follow the instructions you will enjoy an increase in spare money that you are free to enjoy. The pleasure of *Magickal Riches* is that you can enjoy spending money to get the things you want and the life you want to live.

רזיאל

גבריאל סוריאל רומיאל הסדיאל שמריאל
מיכאל רפאל
צדקיאל פניאל
רחמיאל גוריאל
רזיאל יופיאל
יהו יהו יהן יהו יהו
שמשיאל יהואל
אוריאל זכריאל יהואל מלתיאל רזיאל

ידהמובה
ד דודניאל
מ משפידאל
ב ביבאל

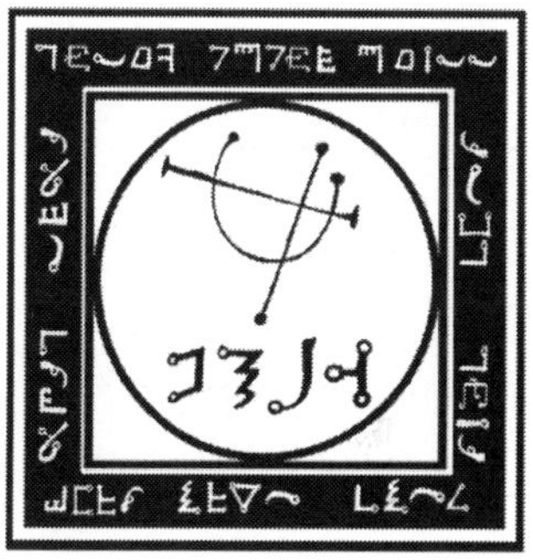

How to Make Money with Magick

Magick works best when you know what you want, and when you don't care exactly when or how your results will manifest.

Money magick requires an additional twist. You will get the best results from this money magick if you focus on the pleasant emotions of spending money and enjoying money, rather than on the emotion of receiving money.

Although you may dream of receiving a large amount of money, that isn't what you really want. You want to *spend* money. You want to *enjoy* money. You want the things that money can bring, rather than money itself. Getting to grips with this concept is essential to fire up your occult money making.

This approach is the exact opposite to the method described in *Magickal Cashbook*. In that book, I describe a technique where you name a specific amount that you want to manifest. That method works well in the context of that particular ritual. For the magick in this book you should not think about the numbers at all. (Feel free to continue with the *Magickal Cashbook* as well, but when using this book, let go of the numbers and concentrate on the pleasure of using plentiful money, instead of receiving a specific amount.)

Rather than thinking about how much money you want, or how you want to get it, you need to think about what you would actually do with your time if you had all the money you ever dreamed of having.

It's hard to believe, but having a lot of money can quickly lead to boredom if you don't know what you really want from life. Having a bank account stuffed with money might make you feel secure for a while, but it doesn't bring joy. Spending money and doing exciting and pleasant things is where the joy comes from. Money can bring you joy, but only when you have found joyous ways of releasing your money.

The first time I had access to a lot of money (by virtue of living with a generous and wealthy young woman) I was unbearably bored, and gave up many hobbies and interests. I even gave up writing fiction for a while. The money had a bad effect on me, because excess money wasn't as enjoyable as I'd imagined it would be. It didn't bring that much relief or security, and it didn't fill the emotional holes that I had hoped it would fill.

We broke up amicably and I soon returned to near-poverty, and in the months that followed I learned what I really wanted to do with my time and how I wanted to live. This is what counts. When it comes to money, this is all that you need to know. *What do you actually want to do with your time?*

When you have money, how will you spend your time on a daily basis? If you could buy whatever you wanted, what would it be? How would you spend your day? Where would you travel and why? If you can answer questions like these, then the money itself doesn't matter.

You're not actually trying to manifest money. You're manifesting the lifestyle, security and pleasure that money can bring. It might sound like there's not much difference, but there is an essential difference that needs to be explored.

Money and Pleasure

I have spoken to countless people about money, and when I ask them what they would do if they won the lottery, many people say that they would buy a new home, a new car, a boat and that they would travel. This is a *reaction*, rather than a well thought-out response to deep and genuine desire.

When I delve a little deeper and ask what sort of home they want and what sort of boat, most people quickly admit that they don't really want the boat after all. A few *do* want a boat, because they have a genuine interest in boats and sailing, but most people realize that it was a dream inflicted on them, rather than a real desire. You see millionaires on TV with boats, so you should have a boat, right? No, you shouldn't. Not unless you like boats.

The same is true of the 'dream home'. Most people imagine that they want a huge mansion, high on a hillside, walled off from the world in complete security, with twenty rooms and more TVs and bathrooms than you can count. The reality of those homes is not what you might think. I have spent time in such homes, and although some people genuinely thrive in them, many people feel lost and overwhelmed by the space, the number of staff required to keep the house operational, the isolation from friends, and the simple inability to find other family members in all those rooms.

This is not to say there's anything wrong with owning a boat or a mansion. You just need to make sure that it would actually make you happy before you go after a dream like that. If you really want a big house, I'm not going to argue. But don't waste your life feeling a sense of lack because you believe the only way to be rich is to have all that stuff.

Owning stuff can be great fun, and buying a dream home or car is a true joy, so long as you're buying something that suits you.

It is easy to get caught up in habits of desire, which can lead you away from your genuine desires. I have seen people buy prestigious inner-city apartments only to discover that they'd rather live on a farm. I have seen many people buy wineries, farms and other large chunks of country real-estate, who then discover that they actually like to live in the city rather than live the country lifestyle. People who go to live on islands rarely make it through a whole year before scrambling back to the mainland, even when they've been dreaming of island-life for decades.

It's all too easy to spend a lot of money and then find out it's been wasted on the wrong dream. A more efficient approach, and a more effective magickal approach, is to find out what brings you pleasure and focus on that. When money becomes less important than the pleasure, it's easier to manifest money.

For a long time I thought I wanted to own an airplane. I used to fly quite regularly, and I wanted my own plane, because that seemed like a much better deal than renting a plane each time I flew. But I discovered that actually owning a plane brings a lot of responsibility. There are decisions about where to hangar the plane, maintenance schedules, and above all else, a sense of guilt when the plane sits unused for a month. Flying shouldn't feel like an obligation, but a joy. So, in truth, I prefer hiring airplanes.

Discovering that about myself was freeing. It saved me a fortune and made me enjoy flying, rather than being burdened. For some people, owning a plane is ideal, and I know several owners who were overjoyed once they owned a good plane. It depends on the individual, and that's why it's so important to delve into your genuine wants and needs.

Enjoying Money Magick

I've seen some people made much happier by just a small increase in money, and other people who don't become happy no matter how much they make. This is why, before you start the actual work of manifestation, you need to think about the pleasure that money would bring you. You will need to focus on how you will spend money, rather than just the feeling of 'being rich'.

A relative of mine dreamed of wealth, but when he eventually landed a job that earned him a high wage, he realized that he didn't actually want all that much after all. He bought a better car, some new clothes and sorted his house out, but he was happy with that. He realized that he'd spent his life dreaming of riches that he didn't need. With about $20,000 more a year, he had all he wanted and felt rich. There was no need for him to burn himself out trying to be a millionaire.

I could tell the same story about many people. A slight increase in money can lead to the lifestyle you want, and you don't have to spend decades being frustrated because you're not a millionaire.

This does not mean you should limit your desires. If being a millionaire is what you genuinely need to fulfill your dreams, then it's within your reach. I am not saying that you should forget about being rich. I am saying that when it comes to money magick, you should focus on the pleasures that money can bring to you, rather than a set amount of money that you think would make you rich.

If you can focus on the pleasures of living with money, you have more chance of getting the magick to work, and more chance of enjoying it when it does work.

The attainment of pleasure is integral to money magick, so work out what gives you pleasure, without even thinking about money. Some people have expensive tastes, and if you do, that's fine, so long as it's really what you want.

To have magickal riches does not mean that you hold on to money, but that you let money flow into your life, and then you enjoy spending it or using it in some way that makes your life better. In some cases, that might mean that you save the money. For some people, saving is a way to enjoy money and it is better than living off credit. It helps if you know what you are saving *for*, though.

Money is only of any real use when you eventually get rid of it. Putting it in a bank account can earn interest and help you to create savings, but eventually, its actual use comes when you *spend* that money. Money enables you to do things, be places and own things, which means you must let go of money as continually as you receive it.

Some of the material goods you desire can bring genuine pleasure, and this is what you should look for. Look for the pleasure. While writing this book I bought a new car, and it was exactly what I wanted in every way. I never get into that car without a small thrill of pleasure. I enjoy driving it, and so that was a beautiful use of money.

There is nothing shallow or unspiritual about wanting material goods. If you want money magick to work, then you need to enjoy your material possessions in this way.

When buying essential goods, or paying bills and taxes, you need to be relaxed about letting go of money, rather than holding onto it tightly. The magick in this book will guide you to be relaxed about money.

The Splendor of Money

Be wary of trying to impress others with money, because that can get in the way of magick.

I once spent an hour with a cab driver in the UK, who spent the entire journey telling me that he worked painfully long hours, but that he spent all his money on designer clothes, jewelry and perfumes for his wife and children. He named label after label, hoping to impress me. I was not impressed.

This man was a tragic figure, desperately buying labels and logos, earned through a life of overwork, so that others would admire him for his apparent wealth. In reality, he was living in poverty and he wasn't fooling anybody. He looked poor and sounded poor, despite his expensive watch.

I later found out where he lived, because my brother knew of him. It was an ugly part of town and an ugly house. He was living a difficult life, in a horrible place, hoping that a few designer products would buy him happiness. He didn't have a shred of happiness about him. Everything about him reeked of desperation.

There is nothing wrong with designer clothes and expensive perfumes, if you get pleasure out of them, but if you sacrifice your precious time, and live in actual poverty, all in the hope of impressing others by putting on a show of wealth, you cannot feel rich.

Being rich is never about getting one over other people or impressing friends and strangers with your wealth. It is about enjoying the life you want to lead.

You may think none of this is a problem for you, because you'd *really* like to win eighty million dollars on the lottery, or you *know* you want to get out of debt, or you are *certain* you want a new car, but it's rarely that simple. Many people have unconscious hang-ups about money that can affect their willingness to receive.

If there's any chance that you might feel guilty about a successful magickal manifestation - because it feels unfair to receive the wealth – that can stop the flow of money.

I had this problem myself. Brought up in a working class family, and often living in quite severe poverty (by Western standards), I was led to believe that money was difficult to obtain and painful to spend. That was my experience. No matter how much I wanted money, I was afraid that it would be difficult to earn and that spending it was a form of loss.

That attitude led to problems. When I lived with the wealthy woman mentioned earlier, I still thought that being rich was in some way unfair, and that added to my inability to enjoy the wealth that was on offer.

It took me a long time to get over my mindset. Only when I accepted that money could appear easily, and that spending it was more fun than holding onto it tightly, did money magick really start to pick up for me.

This doesn't mean you have to convince yourself that money is good and the world is fair and that all rich people are kind, but you may have to do some work to ensure that your ingrained attitudes to money leave you more open to receiving money.

The magick in this book is designed to take the focus off money, and onto pleasure, which will help, but try to ensure that you don't resent those who live a wealthy life.

The Balance of Money

Some people are brought up to think that money is evil, and that the rich are cruel. In some ways, these thoughts are sane and sound. It is outrageous that our world contains a small handful of billionaires, while billions of people live in abject poverty. There are many rich people that exploit workers unfairly, and many hard workers who are never paid well. The world is not fair or balanced.

To obtain money through magick, you are putting out a request for more money than you have now. You are imposing your will on reality, and stating that you want to have more money than many other people. You need to feel comfortable about receiving money and spending money, despite the lack of justice in world economics.

If you are disgusted by the misuse of money, the greed of some billionaires, and the unfairness of poverty, know that you can do more to help that situation when you are wealthy than when you are poor.

Staying poor helps nobody. Allowing money and pleasure into your life makes it easier to help anybody you want to help, starting with yourself.

Whatever else, make sure that you don't resent the rich. If you resent others who have money, you cannot expect to become a person who is at ease with money. I know people of all income levels, and I have to admit that many rich people are repellant to me, because they enjoy looking down on others who are less well off. Such people are not pleasant to be around. But I also know many rich people who love their life, using their money in wonderful ways that bring great pleasure. Being around these people is delightful. It's the same with poor and middle-class people. Plenty are vile, and many are beautiful. In other words, it's the person and their attitude that makes them pleasant, not their actual level of income.

I have encountered people who desperately want to be rich, while hating the rich. Magick will amplify the feelings you put in, so if you go into it with petty resentment and a mean-spirited attitude there's a good chance you will amplify those feelings.

I had a friend who I'd known since school, and even when we lived very different lives we still saw a lot of each other. He didn't believe in magick, but he wanted to do a self-help course on using The Law of Attraction to make money, because he thought that might work for him. He downloaded a pirated copy of the course, because he said it was too expensive to buy. If it worked, he said, he'd pay later. I wasn't sure he was being truthful.

After a few days I pointed out that he'd already spent more money on beer than he'd have spent on the course. He didn't care about that, because he didn't like the idea of paying rich people for the course. In his mind, they were already rich and didn't deserve his money. I didn't waste my time pointing out that wealthy shareholders owned the brewery that made his beer.

I wasn't surprised that he didn't get good results from the course. He went into the process with an attitude of resentment, pettiness, and a deep unwillingness to let go of money. He had a belief that the rich don't deserve their wealth. It was clearly impossible for him to join them.

If you've bought this book, it's because you want more money, but you may have uneasy feelings about people who have money. If so, remember that what you really want is *the results that money can bring*.

You may not know what you want yet, or what experiences will bring you pleasure, and that's OK. Certainty is not required, but self-honesty is, and you should begin to think about why you yearn for more money. Is it just to get by and pay the bills, or because you want security, or something more exciting? There's no right answer, only an honest one.

Whatever your answer may be, it can change over time. Make sure you don't seek more money just because you assume it will make you happier. Extra money rarely makes people happier unless it fulfills another need.

Taking the Money Out of Magick

Your wants and desires do not need to be noble or pious. If you want to travel the world and go nightclubbing for ten years, magick can help with that. If you want enough money to leave your current job and become an artist, it is possible. If you want to collect sports cars, nobody will argue with you. If you want to pay the bills and feel a little more relaxed, that's also a valid goal.

If you use the magick in this book to manifest the things you want to do, and the feelings you want to feel, rather than the money you need to get to that point, then the money will turn up.

If, for example, you want to travel, focus on the emotions of going on that vacation, and the pleasure you would get from being on vacation. You can even focus on the pleasure of booking the vacation and the excitement of planning the trip, if it's too difficult to imagine the vacation itself. Put that energy into your magick, and the money will turn up. If you focus on the $20,000 you *need* to travel, you're much less likely to get results.

Even if somebody owes you exactly $5000, don't perform a ritual to get $5000. Perform a ritual to get the feeling of relief that comes when a debtor pays up.

If you want a new car, don't perform a ritual to get $35,000, but use magick to attract the feeling of having the new car.

If you want an overall increase in the money that flows into your life, don't think about how many tens of thousands extra you want to earn, but think about how it would feel to live the life you want to live.

In short, you take the money out of the magick. Focus on the feelings that more money will bring, and money will come to you. Every ritual in this book will explain how to use this process to get the best results as fast as possible.

Making the Magick Safe

This book does not contain any dark or demonic work. It uses only angelic names, words of power and a group of intelligent spirits that can attract money. The magick has been crafted with safety in mind.

Despite this, I know that many people are afraid that when you perform magick, you always have to pay in some way. You may believe that the spirits require payment, or that the universe will punish you for having too much.

These are common fears, but in thirty-five years of occult experience, I have seen that the opposite is true. When you earn money with magick, it is yours to do with as you please, and there is never any spiritual backlash.

This is because magick can enable you to pursue your true will, and get the pleasures you desire, and because there is no universal balance when it comes to money.

When you look at global economics, without even considering magick, there is nothing fair about the way that money is distributed. People who do the least productive labor often make the most money. People who work with their hands, producing the food and goods we all want and need, earn the least money.

This is blatantly unfair, and yet the rich are never punished, and the poor are never rescued by some inherent sense of universal balance.

Unless you do something about it, the rich remain rich, the middle classes stay exactly where they are, and the poor stay poor.

There is balance in nature, but not in money.

Although this is not an ideal state of affairs, it puts to rest the idea that being wealthy will somehow result in a backlash or a restoration of balance. If you look carefully, you'll notice that wealthy families tend to stay wealthy. If you get rich, you will probably die rich.

When it comes to magick, there are many people who have become rich, or just earned a little extra with money magick, and they have not experienced any backlash.

Do not fear that you will have to pay for the magick in any way. The act of performing magick, putting your energy into the working, and then enjoying the result is the only payment you need.

The final point of that sentence is an important one. You need to enjoy using the money you receive from magick – even if you're only paying bills – for the flow of magickal money to be continuous.

There is nobody judging you for wanting money or for enjoying its benefits. There is no angel sitting on high, judging your desires and labeling you as greedy. If you use magick to obtain the life you want, there is no karmic punishment awaiting you. The only danger is guilt. If you feel guilty about making money with magick, you may stop the flow of money. This is another reason that it's important to get comfortable with your wants and needs.

You may want a lot or you may only want a little, and there is no right or wrong. I live a life that many would consider excessive and greedy. Others look at me and wonder why I only own two cars when I could afford more. It's different for everybody, so focus on what you want, rather than what you think you should want. If you know you'll enjoy the money that comes to you, then it will manifest continually when you use this magick.

Emotional Alchemy

During the rituals you will undergo a process of emotional change. Rather than focusing on the positive emotions that you want to achieve, magick involves a moment of alchemy, where you allow one emotion to change into another. You may, for example, change a feeling of lack to a feeling of having what you want.

During a ritual to attract more money, you do not merely focus on the emotion of having money and enjoying money. Instead, you begin by acknowledging past pain regarding money, noticing your current feelings toward money, and allow those feelings to transmute into something more pleasant as the ritual progresses.

This transmutation of feelings is nothing more than an act of imagination, but it is the most potent fuel for magickal work. If you can imagine how good it would feel to have a result come about, and experience that moment of pleasure as though it has already happened, your magick will take the emotion and manifest it as a result in the real world.

The act of willfully changing your emotions with imagination, combined with the structure of the ritual, creates the magickal effect. By changing your emotions during a ritual, reality is compelled to fall into place.

In some cases, you use memory to generate emotions, and in other cases you use imagined situations. Some rituals work with imagined archetypal situations that generate the required emotions.

Do not overlook the role of emotion in these rituals. If you follow all the instructions correctly, but neglect to do the emotional work embedded within the ritual, you will not get results.

You'll be relieved to know that this takes no great effort. You know what you want, and you can imagine how it would feel to have it, and that is what you need for this magick to work. Each ritual will provide instructions to guide you on the best way to acknowledge, experience and transmute your emotions to get the results you want.

How Your Money Will Manifest

When you use the magick in this book, expect the money to manifest in unusual ways. Do not try to predict where or when the money will come from. You may be surprised at the variety of inventive ways the spirits have for bringing money into your life.

When working with the occult you are advised not to lust for results. That is, if you let go of the result, and don't check anxiously to see where and when it will manifest, it will manifest more readily. If you doubt and fear and monitor your results too closely, or assume the magick has failed, that can interrupt the magick and prevent it from working.

It is never a good idea to say 'that ritual didn't work' until at least a year has passed, because you just don't know where or when the result will manifest. When you declare your magick a failure, you're cancelling the magick out. Give the magick time. This magick is designed to work fast, but magick takes the path of least resistance. Sometimes, the easiest way to manifest a specific result is by waiting for the right time. I have done magick to recover debts, and sometimes I have been paid within hours, while at other times it has taken over a year, but I didn't care, because at least I got the money.

If all the magick in this book took a year to work, it wouldn't be much use to you, so fear not, you should get some very fast results, but don't sit around waiting for them. Allow the results to come about when they come about.

When you've seen results occur a few times, this will rarely be an issue for you, but when starting out you may be extremely eager to see a result. This eagerness can come from a desire for proof that the magick works, or simply because you need the money right now. That's perfectly understandable, but the best approach is to adopt the mindset that magick works when you give it the time and space to work. The less you rush it, the faster it happens. The less you care about a result, the better the result will be.

Being this relaxed about results does take some mental skill, but you don't have to pretend to be desireless. Of course you want money, and of course you want the results you're aiming for in this book. You have genuine wants and a real desire for money. You almost certainly want it right now. So how are you meant to cope with the paradox?

In practice this means that every time you think about a ritual that you've already performed – which may be once a day, or fifty times a day – don't worry about the result or concern yourself with any lack you may feel. Instead, remember the moment of emotional alchemy, and the emotion you were left with at the end of the ritual. This takes just a moment. You refocus on the final emotion, and the pleasure that you imagine you'll feel when the result comes about. And then you busy yourself with something else, rather than wondering where the money will come from.

If you find that you are focusing on lack, or worrying about a result, ease yourself away from the thought, and distract yourself with some other activity. A few stray thoughts will not hijack your magick. It's only when you obsessively worry and hope for a result that you can dampen the magickal effect.

Hope is another form of doubt. Whenever you hope, you are underlining your doubt. One of the wonderful things about magick is that you don't need belief or faith for the magick to work. I've seen people who don't believe in angels get great results from angelic magick, because they followed the steps correctly. Doubt, though, can undermine your efforts, as can hope.

Instead of hoping, doubting, wishing or praying, you should approach magick with casual confidence. Perform the magick seriously, with focused intent, but then get on with your life as though you never did the magick at all.

You can even complete a ritual and then assume that it might take as long as a year for the result to manifest. That way, you let go, you stop hoping, and you stop wishing for a quick payment. If you can trick yourself into thinking like that, you'll get some pleasant surprises.

It's also important to do your part in the real world. If you perform a gambling ritual, make sure you at least buy a lottery ticket. If you're doing magick to recover debt, don't stop legal proceedings to recover the debt. Instead, push ahead with the legal work harder than ever. If you're doing money to attract more sales, do all the real world work you can to improve your sales. The more you do in the real world, the greater the magickal impact. Your efforts accelerate the magick, and the magick empowers your efforts.

For some of these rituals there isn't much you can do. The Master Money Ritual, for example, only requires that you remain open to moments of intuition, and that you welcome unexpected money.

When money does come to you, out of the blue, never dismiss it as coincidence. Magick usually works by arranging a series of coincidences to get you what you want.

If you perform a ritual to get a debt paid, and the money arrives in an envelope an hour later, you might be tempted to think, 'It can't have been the magick, because this was posted yesterday and I only just did the ritual.' Magick works through both directions in time. You can affect events in the past, to align with the future you want. This is why magick can sometimes yield a result within minutes. When you get a magickal result, enjoy it, and know that your magick has worked.

It is clear that you should not lust for result, but you should never ignore results when they come. The act of enjoying a result is vital if you want your magick to work on a continual basis. Celebrate your results, even the small ones, and greater things will come to pass.

The Act of Magick

The act of performing magick generates magickal power. The act of saying words, transmuting your feelings and using your imagination (no matter how poor your imagination may be) creates magickal energy. This is why so many people get results from books such as *Words of Power* without having to go into a trance or spend years being initiated into magick. Doing magick creates the energy of magick.

Although this is true, people often ask me how they can increase their magickal power. I have tried to simplify the magick in my books so that the rituals work without any great energy or ceremony. Even so, I understand that you may want to put extra magickal power into your work. When it comes to money magick, this is a wise approach.

This part of the book offers a technique that helps to build magickal energy that can be used in all occult workings. When used correctly this technique does not drain you, but adds energy to your work without any strain on you, because you are drawing energy from the infinite.

In each ritual, there will come a point where you are told to create *Light From The Dark*, and that is the technique explored in this chapter. For the sake of clarification, it involves contemplating infinity, and does not in any way refer to black magick.

You can, at this point, skip ahead and start on a ritual immediately if you want to – leaving out this step from each ritual - but you will probably want to come back to this section to ensure that you are giving your magick everything you can. Although the rituals will work without this additional technique, it does give the workings more power, so it is worth taking the time to get used to this practice.

If it's so powerful, why is it optional? This technique is a little more advanced than some, and requires a good degree of concentration, focus and imagination. Although you may get it right straight away, it could take some time to develop it fully. You are free to start working on rituals, while you build up the ability to use this technique. That's not to say that this is difficult, but some people find that it takes time to get it working as clearly as they want. Although I don't believe in rushing into magick, I don't think you should spend weeks practicing this energy-work when you could get straight into the magick. My advice is to attempt the following *Light From The Dark* technique. If it's difficult, then keep practicing, but start on your first ritual as soon as you like, leaving this step out. If you find it easy, then you can start using it within a ritual as soon as you want. If you find it quite easy, but not extremely easy, spend a short while getting used to it, but feel free to perform some rituals in the meantime.

This technique took many years to develop. The original idea was passed down to Gordon Winterfield - one of the oldest members of The Gallery of Magick - and we set about making it more workable. We have now crafted something simple enough that we can share it with you.

The technique does require a degree of visualization, but don't worry if you are not able to visualize clearly. Some people can only visualize hazy, faded images. Others can see everything in crystal clear 3D. Some people see no images at all. That is fine. If I tell you to imagine a ball of light, you can imagine a ball of light even without any visual imagination. You can simply *know* that it exists, or say the words, 'There is a ball of light,' in your head.

I mention this because I know that for some people visualization is as natural as memory, but for others it seems like an impossible task. Whatever imagination you possess will be sufficient for this technique to work.

If you've read a few magickal texts you will know that many authors talk about channeling energy through your body. There are hundreds of books exploring chakras and similar ideas, along with the famous Middle Pillar exercise, which involves a comparable process. In almost all of these workings you are told to imagine light moving through your body, while creating glowing spheres at various points inside your body. This technique works, but what I like about the *Light From The Dark* approach, is that you don't try to imagine light. Instead, you contemplate darkness and discover the light that arises from infinite space.

This may sound quite esoteric, but it can quickly become a practical technique.

You can practice this technique outside of ritual, to become familiar with its workings. You may want to close your eyes, although some people find it easier to keep their eyes open. Experiment to see what works best for you. You can sit, stand or lie down.

Take a moment to become aware of your body, and notice the sensations that you can feel.

Move your attention to the inside of your chest, but instead of picturing the organs and bones, imagine a vast empty space within you. It's as though you are looking at an empty, black space the size of the universe. Do not put in too much effort or strain into picturing this. Allow your awareness of this dark emptiness to arise.

If you feel nothing or see nothing, simply pretend. This may sound ridiculous, but pretending is not all that different to visualizing, and if you pretend there's an empty space inside you, it has the same effect. Magick is not meant to feel ordinary, and that means you may have to step outside of your mental comfort zone slightly.

An alternate approach - that some people use to great effect - is to actually imagine the universe within your body. Picture a mass of galaxies and billions of stars, and then snuff the image out, leaving the vast emptiness within you.

Whatever approach you use, you may experience nothing, or you may sense a strange sensation of being within the darkness at the same time as observing it from outside. Whatever you experience is fine.

As you watch this enormous empty space within your body, allow light to arise within the space. This should not be a star of light, or a pinprick, but a gradual lightening of the dark, as though an even, white haze is brightening the entire space. Allow this to brighten and brighten, until it is a glaring white light.

In most cases, you will not need to pretend, imagine or force this to happen. When you contemplate the darkness within you, the light will gradually arise all by itself. It should take less than a minute, but you may find it takes up to five minutes. If you do not see the light arising spontaneously, then use your imagination to start this off.

Remember that you aren't just picturing this; you are picturing it happening in a vast space within your body. You may find that the light extends through your entire body, including your head, hands and feet. Some people even find that it extends beyond their body. Again, whatever you experience is fine.

Once you have created the light, you can direct it into a ritual as follows.

When you can see or feel the light within you, let it pour out of you into the sigil or talisman that's being used in the ritual. You can allow the light to burst out of your chest, flow out of your fingertips, or beam from your eyes. Some people feel the light leave them in one rush, while others sense it seeping out slowly. It might emerge from your forehead, in a breath, or from every pore in your skin. There is no correct way to do this. You can choose a technique in advance, or just allow something to happen at this point, and discover how the light emerges from you. It may be different every time, but most people find that one method works best for them. Whatever method you use, this should be effortless. You allow the light to leave you and move into the talisman or sigil. You do not need to force it out of yourself. Instead, let it leave you, and know that it has energized the working.

If you're using a ritual that contains several sigils, ensure that you only use a small burst of light on each one, so that you have sufficient energy for all of them.

In each of the rituals you will be shown exactly when to build up the *Light From The Dark*, and when to release it.

When you are practicing this technique, rather than using it within a ritual proper, you can simply let the light dissipate. Do not try to extinguish it, but allow it to spread out and fade away, like thinning fog. It may take a minute or so for the light to fade and for you to settle back into the real world fully.

It's important to know that you are not using your own magickal energy when you create *Light From The Dark*. You are not forcing something into existence, so much as recognizing power and energy that is already present, focusing on it, and letting it flow into your magick.

The Master Money Ritual

This ritual is designed to attract more money on an ongoing basis. It works as a standalone ritual, but can also add power to all the other money magick that you perform.

On a trip to the Middle East in 2010, several members of The Gallery of Magick visited an exhibition displaying magickal artifacts and manuscripts. We gathered a great deal of information on that trip, but perhaps the paramount discovery was a pair of talismans from the manuscript of *Hokhmat ha-Kabbalah ha-Ma'asit*. The Hebrew letter combinations in those talismans are enormously powerful. For some time, we used the talismans in their original form.

Two years later, we began developing our own talisman, by taking the letter combinations from both talismans, combining them into one image, and arranging them according to a secret pattern. The pattern is designed to attract wealth.

Our talisman is displayed in this chapter and contains the secret letter circles, along with associated words of power and angelic names. When empowered by ritual, this talisman can attract an increase in the money that you are able to enjoy.

It works by breaking down barriers to prosperity, alerting you to opportunity and making you somebody who attracts money.

This ritual may seem long and complex, but it is surprisingly simple. It may take you a short while to learn all the steps, but once you know them, the ritual can be carried out in a few minutes.

When you first use this ritual, perform it once each day for eleven days. You can then repeat it every few months, but when you repeat it you only need to perform it for three days in a row. Some people feel an urge to repeat this ritual after two months, and that is fine. In general, however, you should get good results if you repeat this every three or four months. Remember, you only need to do the full eleven days the very first time you use the ritual. After that, three days is all you need. If money is flowing steadily, you might only need to do the three-day ritual once a year.

When you begin, you can perform the ritual for eleven consecutive days, or if that's impossible, you can spread the eleven days out over several weeks. Ideally, you should not leave more than two days between each ritual. So if you perform it on a Friday, but can't work on it over the weekend, try to get started again on the Monday. If that's impossible, due to your personal circumstances, you will still get results, but make sure you get all eleven days performed within one month.

When you repeat the working a few months later, try to find a time when you can work the ritual for three days in a row, without interruption.

This ritual involves getting into a certain state of mind, saying words of power, using emotional energy and magickal energy, as well as scanning your eyes over the sigil. The sigil is comprised of many Hebrew letters, but you don't need to be able to read Hebrew to get this to work.

If you're curious about what the words say, most of them are divine names, words of power, angelic names and other words that call on prosperity. The letters in the circles are beyond translation. This form of magick often uses acronyms, codes and patterns to create the desired effect, making it something that can't be translated.

The main sigil looks like this:

The sigil is displayed in a larger form later in the book.

When I describe the full ritual, you will be asked to scan the letters. This means that you pass your eyes over the letters, looking at their shapes. You do not attempt to read or understand them. Even if you can read Hebrew easily, there is no need to read the words. Look at the shapes of the letters with relaxed eyes, and know that the letter shapes are sinking into your consciousness.

You need to perform this scanning in a specific pattern, and the next few pages will help you to learn this. It might take you a little bit of practice to get this right. You can practice this technique freely, and it will not activate the talisman. Do not worry that by looking at the letters you might activate the talisman inadvertently. Only when you come to the ritual and deliberately activate it, will the effects begin to occur.

To begin, look at the vertical word on the left – where it says 'Step 1 Start

Here', scan your eyes from the bottom of the word to the top. You do not need to rotate your book or device. Simply scan your eyes up the word, all the way to the top (where the head of the arrow ends). Now move your eyes across to the word on the right, for Step 2, and scan down, until you scan the final letter near the head of the arrow.

For Step 3, start on the right and scan your eyes across the line of highlighted letters until you reach the point marked by the head of the arrow.

Move your eyes to the place where it says, 'Step 4 Start Here'. Scan your eyes across the first two words, from right to left, following the direction of the arrow. Move down to the next line, and again scan from right to left. Keep moving down a line at a time, until you have scanned all six lines of text in this section.

For Step 5, move your eyes to the far right, at the bottom of the image, and scan the letters of these five words, from right to left, as indicated by the arrow.

For Step 6 you move your eyes up to the outer white circle, and scan your eyes anticlockwise around the circle, three times. It's important to start on the top right, where the arrowhead points, and then continue in an anticlockwise manner. Don't worry if you accidentally see other letters, but you should aim to begin your scan at this point on the circle.

As you move your eyes anticlockwise around this circle, you will be looking at some letters that are upside-down, and that is fine. You are not reading, but letting the letter shapes sink in, so continue this slow scanning, moving your eyes anticlockwise, taking in the shape of each letter. When you have done this three times you can move on to the next circle.

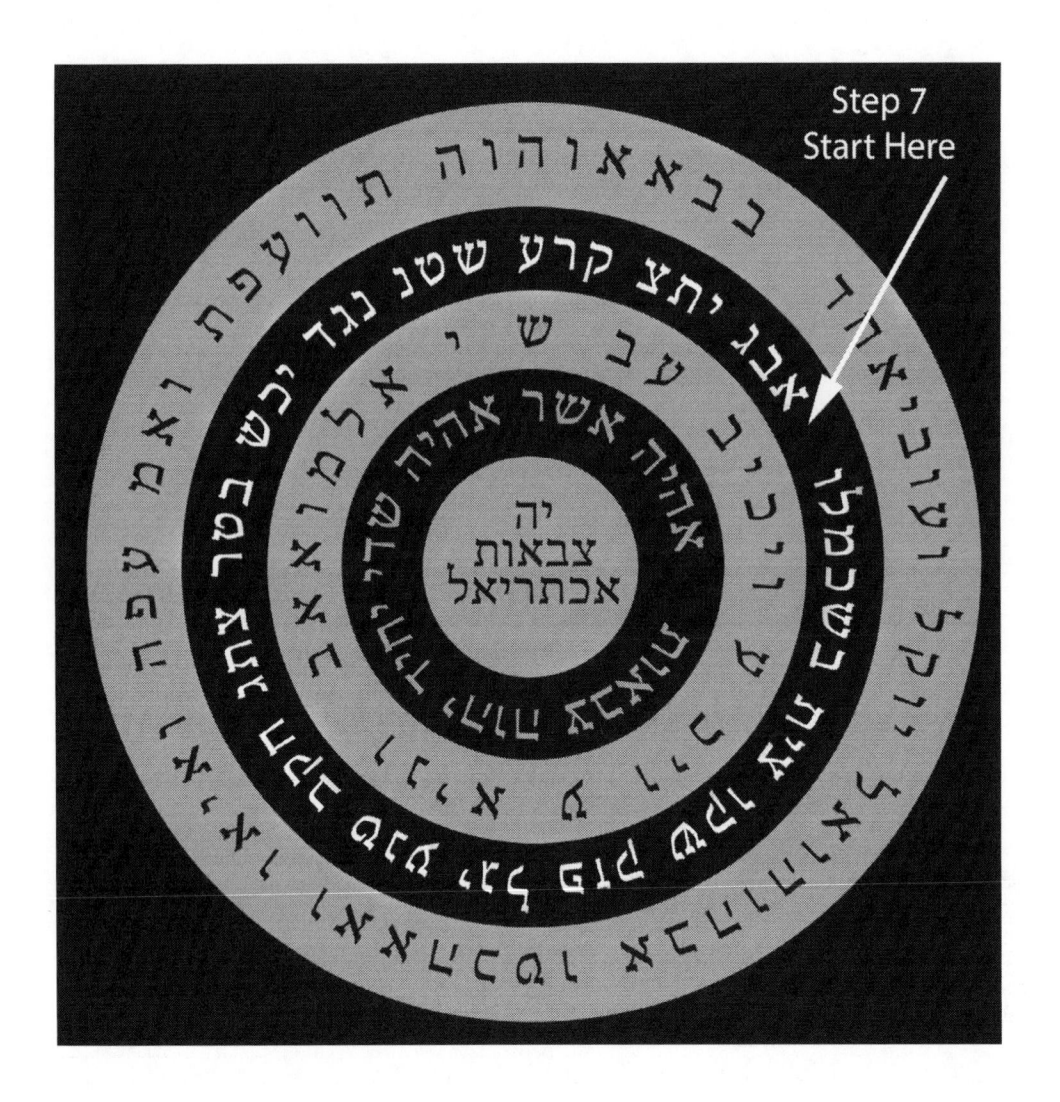

For Step 7, move in to the next circle, and begin scanning anticlockwise from the point shown by the head of the arrow. Again, scan these letters three times. You may find that you begin to see other letters, or even the whole sigil, out of the corner of your eye. That happens all the time, and is nothing to worry about. So long as you pass your eyes over the letters as instructed, the correct letter shapes will be absorbed.

When it comes to Step 8, you move to the next circle in, but this time you start on the bottom left. Again, move your eyes around the circle in an anticlockwise direction, three times.

Move to the next circle inward, for Step 9, and begin the scan at the head of the arrow, moving anticlockwise around the circle three times. If you're unfamiliar with these letters it may take some practice to remember where these starting points are. If you look closely, you'll see that there is a slightly larger gap between the words at each of these starting points. That gap can help you to locate the starting point when you are learning how to use this talisman.

When you come to the central circle, you are looking at a list of three words. Starting with the uppermost word, scan the two letters from right to left. Move down to the next word and scan the letters from right to left. Move down to the lower word, and scan the letters from right to left. Finally, allow yourself to see the circle itself, taking in its shape. You may or may not be aware of the letters contained within the circle at this point.

The final scan is not a letter scan, but a way of taking in the entire sigil. Start at the top, in the exact center, as shown, and scan down. Keep moving your eyes down, until you reach the base. This should not take more than five seconds, because it is a scan, rather than an attempt to see everything in detail.

When you scan the letters during the ritual, you also need to imagine a fiery light arising from the sigil. If you can visualize at all, then as you scan over the letters, let a fiery light - like the light you see in a fire - burn through all the white parts of the image. The light can be a steady glow, or can flicker like a flame. If you struggle with visualization, simply know there is a fiery light around the letters.

When you scan white letters against a black background, picture the white letters as glowing or burning with fire. When you scan black letters against a white background, you scan the letters and see them surrounded by the glowing light. In short, all the white parts of the image are turned to yellow-orangey fire with your imagination.

Do not put too much effort into this. Is should not be a strain. You will find that it becomes easier with time, and whatever visualization skills you have will be sufficient.

What if you're using an e-book? It's perfectly acceptable to use the talisman as it is presented later in this chapter, without the need for anything to be physically printed out. If you're using a physical copy of the book, you can use the sigil as shown in the book, or photocopy the image and use that. It is your perception of the image and your imagination that makes it effective, so it doesn't matter whether it exists on a screen, page or a piece of paper.

Once you're familiar with the correct scanning pattern, and this addition of the colored light, you can start work on the ritual itself.

With the talisman in front of you, remember a time when you felt a great lack, or some kind of poverty or pain. As discussed in the first part of the book, this should not be an emotion about money itself – such as losing money, or getting a wage cut – but an emotion about your life and experience when there wasn't enough money. It's a subtle difference, but an important one. If you lost your wallet and couldn't buy dinner, don't think about the money you lost, but think about how hungry you were when you missed out on dinner.

This doesn't have to be a traumatic memory, or even a clear one, but it should be a memory that makes you recall the feeling of being without the things you wanted or needed. It could be a distant memory, or something from this morning. It might be the same memory every time you perform the ritual or something different. All you are trying to do is attain a state where you recognize the feeling of lack.

Avoid putting words or judgments on this feeling. Try not to think about how or why the situation came about, or who was to blame, but focus on the pure emotion. For example, I often remember a time when I was living in a cold house, and when the heating broke my landlord refused to pay for repairs. I couldn't afford to get the work done, so I felt clear, obvious lack. When using this memory, I don't focus on my anger at the landlord, and I certainly don't focus on how empty my bank account was at the time. Instead, I focus on the sensation of feeling utterly bereft because I couldn't get myself the comfort I wanted. I focus on feeling cold and unable to get out of that situation.

I have plenty of mildly amusing memories involving poverty, but those are not ideal for this process. It's best to remember something that stirs a slightly unpleasant feeling. The key here is to find a memory that involves the feeling of poverty, without actually focusing on the lack of money.

Ideal memories would be:

- A time when you couldn't afford food. You'd focus on the hunger, not the lack of money.

- When your car broke because you couldn't afford repairs. You focus on the feeling of owning an inferior and broken car, not the money you needed to repair it.

- The time you couldn't pay the rent. You focus on the fear of being evicted, rather than the fact that you didn't have money for the rent.

- A trip you wanted to take, that never came to fruition. Focus on the feeling of having missed out, rather than on why you couldn't afford it.

As you can see, there are many different ways to approach this, but always focus on the emotional experience that was brought about by a lack of money. You may want to plan ahead and work out an effective memory before diving into the ritual. Some people prefer to hunt for a memory while in the ritual. This is a matter of personal preference.

Whatever memory you use, it is important that you experience the emotion all over again, as though it is happening now. Let the feeling arise, and sit with this feeling, without judgment. Observe it and acknowledge that the pain or discomfort in the memory is real.

You now speak a series of names and words that call on angelic aid, to bring relief from lack. There are many angelic names listed in this talisman, but this short series of words ends with the name of Metatron, binding the sigil to the power of this mighty archangel.

Ideally, you should say these words out loud, spoken with calm authority and a clear voice. If you cannot say the words out loud, due to privacy issues, imagine the sound of the words, and imagine that you are calling to the ends of the universe. Know that as you say the words you are attracting the attention of the many angels that are named in the talisman.

Here are the words you say:

EE-AH

TZ-VAH-OTT

ACH-AT-REE-ELL

YOT-ZAF-CHEE-RON

MET-A-TRON

A full pronunciation guide is included in the Appendix. Most of the sounds are just like English, except for the CH sound, which is like the *ch* in the Scottish *loch* or the German *achtung*. See the pronunciation guide for more details.

Having said the words, you now transmute the emotion. In the earlier part of the book you were shown how to find feelings of abundance, prosperity and wealth, by focusing on the results of money, rather than on money itself. At this point in the ritual, you allow your emotions to change from the feeling of lack to the feeling of having or enjoying something (that would be achieved by having money, but without thinking about the money.)

Do not use a memory, but invent something new. Do not imagine something that is simply pleasant, such as spending time with your family. Instead, imagine something that would bring you joy, but something that could only be achieved by having more money. The purpose of this exercise is to create emotion, rather than to aim for an actual result that you want to manifest.

You might, for example, imagine the pleasure of driving a new car. You focus on the pleasure of driving, not on the money required to own the car. If you focus on a vacation, feel the pleasure of being on that vacation, without thinking about where the money came from.

Each time you perform the ritual you can use the same imagined outcome, or you can use something different every time if that helps to generate more emotion. It's important to know that you are simply creating a feeling. You are not actually trying to make this specific future come to pass, although it may well do so. When choosing something to think about, you are free to dream big. Whatever you think about should make you feel good, whether you actually think it is possible or not.

In some cases, you may get the most pleasure from thinking about a reality that is possible and within reach. If a shopping trip to buy new clothes would bring you great pleasure at this point in your life, that might be more effective than imagining yourself living in a mansion. Use the images and ideas that generate the best feelings for you.

You may even want to think about something that is very close to the subject of money. If, for example, you are badly in debt, and want to clear your credit card debt and pay your bills, you might get the most pleasure from being out of debt and paying those bills. This would probably give you more joy than an imagined vacation that feels impossible. If that's the case, then go ahead and imagine a debt-free life. But you should still do this without thinking about the money. So rather than thinking about paying off the debt or paying the bills, you can picture your credit card statement at 0, and all your bills stamped with the word PAID. Feel the pleasure of being out of debt and free, rather than thinking about paying the debt off.

It's important to remember that you are not trying to actually create a specific future here. You are only transmuting emotion, so what you imagine here is only meant to make you feel good, as though you already have plenty of money. As such, you can imagine things that feel truly impossible, or things that may come to pass. There is absolutely no harm in picturing things that you want to happen. If you want to travel the world, picture yourself travelling the world. If you want to buy a new car, picture that. These things may come to pass, but within the context of this ritual these imagined realities are being used purely to make you feel good.

When you transmute your emotion, it's important to imagine the feeling as though the pleasant experience is happening right now. Rather than thinking, 'It would be so wonderful to have a new car,' imagine how it feels to have the car now, as you get in and drive away. Rather than thinking, 'I would love to climb a mountain in Canada,' imagine your exhilaration as you reach the top of that mountain, as though it's happening now. Make the emotion feel completely real, as though it's happening now. This does require active imagination, but it is essential to get this magick to work.

Although this is quite a lengthy description, you may find that you can generate the required emotions in one or two seconds. For others, it takes a few minutes of picturing an imaginary pleasure for the emotions to arise. As soon as the emotion of pleasure has taken away the feeling of lack, you can begin to scan the letters in the talisman as instructed.

Remember to add the fiery light to the letters as you scan, and hold on to the emotion of pleasure. You do not need to remember or recall the images you were using, but try to keep the feeling of pleasure and attainment with you as you scan the letters.

When you have finished the letter scan, you transmute the feeling from pleasure to gratitude. Feel grateful that you are able to experience such pleasure. Again, avoid all thoughts of money, and don't think about what's really going on in your life. You are actively imagining a state where you have what you want, and you feel grateful for the experience. You are not feeling grateful for money, but grateful for the rich experiences you are able to enjoy.

Now repeat the words from earlier, and as you do so feel a surge of gratitude.

Say:

EE-AH
TZ-VAH-OTT

ACH-AT-REE-ELL
YOT-ZAF-CHEE-RON
MET-A-TRON

Use the technique to create *Light From The Dark*. You can let your emotions settle completely at this point. You may find that the positive feelings linger, but there is no need to hold on to them. Instead, focus on creating light from the darkness.

When you have created the light, let it spill into the talisman. You do not need to think about pleasure, money or anything else. At this point, your magickal energy is neutral, and you are merely adding energy to the talisman.

When you sense that you have empowered the talisman, know that the ritual is over. It might help to say, 'It is done,' and then you close the book and distract yourself with something non-magickal. Most people find it's a good idea to cook, talk, read or do something that stops you from dwelling on the magick that you just performed.

Given that this is quite a lengthy description, what follows is a summary of the steps, to help you plan out the ritual. Make sure you have read the chapter thoroughly before using this summary.

- Become familiar with the technique for creating *Light From The Dark*.

- Become familiar with scanning the letter patterns, as described.

- To begin the ritual, contemplate the emotion of lack, using memory.

- Say:

EE-AH
TZ-VAH-OTT
ACH-AT-REE-ELL
YOT-ZAF-CHEE-RON
MET-A-TRON

- Transmute the emotion, by imagining pleasure as though it is happening to you right now.

- Remain aware of the emotion as you scan the letter patterns in the talisman, seeing the fiery light.

- Allow the emotion to make its final alchemical change to gratitude.

- Feeling gratitude, say:

EE-AH
TZ-VAH-OTT
ACH-AT-REE-ELL
YOT-ZAF-CHEE-RON
MET-A-TRON

- Create *Light From The Dark* and pour your energy into the talisman.

- Allow yourself to do something non-magickal, and forget about the magick you have performed.

- The first time you use the ritual, repeat this for eleven days in a row if possible. (Otherwise, perform the ritual on eleven days within one month of starting out.)

- Repeat the ritual for three consecutive days every few months.

The talisman appears at full size on the next page. This is the one you should use during the ritual.

גבריאל סודיאל רומיאל חסדיאל שמריאל
מיכאל רפאל
צדקיאל פניאל
רחמיאל נוריאל
רזיאל יופיאל
יהו יהו יהו יהו יהו
שמשיאל יחואל

אוריאל זכריאל יהואל מלטיאל רזיאל

Discover Your Secret Source of Money

You have a secret source of money waiting to be tapped. All you have to do is find out where this money is. The ritual in this chapter will explain how you can become aware of this secret source of money.

Why is this money a secret? Nobody is deliberately hiding money from you, but the habits of thought, lifestyle and belief that you have developed may keep you separate from many easy sources of income. With the help of the archangel Metatron, you can discover intuitive hints about where this money will come from. This might not sound as exciting as a lottery win, but it can be an extremely lucrative way to make extra money.

In some cases you may discover a new skill that can help supplement your income. At other times, you may realize that you have a helpful relative that is happy to share money around. You may find a new way of selling something you already have, or gain access to funds that were previously out of reach.

When I first used this magick, it gave me an enjoyable surprise. I never saw myself as a professional artist, and painted as a hobby, but after performing this ritual I decided that I should try to sell my art. I was in my early twenties, hanging around with a bunch of art students, and I got a favor from a friend at a gallery. It wasn't a major gallery, but more of a corner of the local arts center. That meant my friend could slip my paintings in there without the upper management having any idea that I was a complete unknown. And my paintings sold. Whenever I exhibited a painting, it sold quickly, while other paintings by more reputable artists stayed on the walls for months at a time. I made more money from a handful of paintings than I had ever made through hard work. I'd discovered a secret source of money, and one that I still enjoy playing with every now and then.

That was not the only discovery. In the early days of Photoshop, back in the nineties, hardly anybody knew how to use it, but a friend of mine showed me the basics. Back in those days, you could earn a small fortune retouching photographs. It's the sort of work that kids do to correct images on their iPads these days, but for a short while it was a highly rewarding side-job. I had to learn a few new skills, but it took a matter of hours. There was no major investment of time or money. I had to put in some time and effort, but the rewards were far greater than those I got from my main job at the time.

Most of the time this magick manifests an intuition that leads you to earning more money, by doing something new, aside from your real job. Sometimes it works by making a friend or relative become generous with money. This hasn't happened to me very often, but some people find that wealthy relatives become more interested in sharing their fortunes once this ritual has been performed.

It's rare for this working to increase your success in an already established area. I was already working as a writer when I found success with this ritual, but none of the success came from writing. (I used other magick for my writing career.) The reason we call this a secret source of money, is that there are many ways that money can come to you, but you need a ritual working such as this to discover them.

I suggest performing this ritual every day for nine days, and then perform it on one day each month. It doesn't matter if you miss a month, or even a year, but if you keep using this ritual once a month you are more likely to get results. Although you can get an instant response, I find that you get the best results when you treat this as a long term, ongoing project. Archangels are extremely powerful and can work rapidly, but if you put in patient commitment you are more likely to discover some unexpected sources of money.

You will need to become familiar with the following sigil:

As with the Master Money Ritual, you will scan the letters visually, rather than trying to read them. The following pages show you the order in which to scan the letter shapes.

In this ritual you do not imagine colored light, but you do picture a glowing light - like bright starlight - coming from the white parts of the image. When you read black letters against white, let the white light shine around the letters. When you read white letters on black, the bright starlight should shine through the white letters.

First, become familiar with the scanning pattern.

Starting at Step 1, scan the letters from right to left (anticlockwise) across the top of the circle.

For Step 2, scan your eyes clockwise around the circle, starting at the head of the arrow, and continuing clockwise (or from the right of the circle to the left), until you've scanned the opposite side of the circle.

In Step 3 you scan the letters from right to left, ending at the head of the arrow.

For Step 4 scan your eyes across the uppermost horizontal word, from right to left. Then for Step 5 move down to the next line of three words, and scan those from right to left.

Read the angelic script from right to left

In Step 6 you scan your eyes over the letters of angelic script that make up the center of the sigil. This is the name of Metatron, written in an angelic alphabet, using just six letters.

Scan from right to left, a little slower than usual, pausing on each letter to see it clearly, and letting the white starlight shine through the letters.

The ritual itself is similar to the Master Money Ritual, but is a little simpler. Begin by performing the scan as described above.

This ritual then involves a visualization that helps to generate the feelings. Imagine that you are in a dark forest at night, and contemplate the feeling of being lost. Don't try to create a sense of drama or panic, but the simple feeling that you are unable to find your way out of the forest, no matter what direction you walk.

If you cannot visualize this clearly, you can say, 'I am walking through a dark forest at night. I am lost,' and other similar phrases. This should help to generate the feeling of being lost.

As with all the rituals in this book, the focus is on emotion, not money. The structure of the ritual, and the formulation of the sigil, makes it clear to Metatron that you want the result to come in the form of secret sources of money, even though you do not focus on money at all.

When you have created this sensation of being lost in the forest, repeat the name MET-A-TRON three times, while gazing casually at the sigil. You do not need to scan the letters or imagine the white light at this point.

Now imagine that you see a beautiful box on the forest floor, made of dark, hard wood. The box opens easily and inside there is bright white light. As you look at the light it turns golden, filling your vision and obscuring the forest. The light then fades away and you see that you are no longer in the forest, but standing in a beautiful open field, watching a golden sunrise.

Transmute the feeling to one of joy – joy that you have found your way out of the forest so easily. Again, if you cannot visualize, or if you struggle to feel these emotions, you can just say the words, 'I see a dark wooden box, and when I open it, the box is filled with white light. The light brightens to a golden light, and then I'm in an open field, far from the forest, and the sun is rising.' If you *can* visualize clearly, there's no need to say these words.

This ritual is unlikely to generate huge emotions, as it is not based on memory, or anything that happens on a daily basis (unless you happen to live in a forest and have a bad sense of direction). It is a form of pathworking, and uses images that generate subtle, archetypal emotions.

You may not feel much at all, or you may feel quite distinct pleasure at seeing the sunrise.

Now use the *Light From The Dark* ritual, as instructed earlier, and pour your energy into the talisman. The working is complete.

Although you are seeking moments of intuition, do not look for them or try to discover your secret source of money. When the ritual is complete, distract yourself with non-magickal activities.

Be ready to write down any flashes of intuition you may receive in the coming days and weeks. Earlier in the book I said that it's important to do as much real world work as you can. In the case of this ritual you can't actively stimulate intuition, but you must be ready to record any ideas or insights that occur to you.

Not every idea will be a gem, but many will, and by keeping a written record you may start to see patterns to your insights. A written record also makes sure that you don't forget a great idea. Don't be tempted to think that a great idea is unforgettable. Almost all writers, artists, inventors and composers talk about ideas they didn't bother to write down, which were forgotten minutes or hours later. The same is true of magickal insights. If you write them down, more will come to you. If you forget them, they will dry up.

The talisman appears at full size on the next page. This is the one you should use during the ritual.

אהיה אשר אהיה

אדירירון

שמועיאל מטטרין יהואל

פזק שקו צית בשכמלו

אבג יתץ קרע שטן נגד יכש בטר צתג חקב שקו צית בשכמלו

Ritual to Increase Sales

If you sell anything, this ritual can increase your sales. It works for sales people aiming for commissions, those selling a product through a business, authors selling books, artists selling paintings and musicians selling albums. Whether you deal with people directly as a salesperson, or simply make your product available online or in a shop, when you have sales figures, this ritual can make them increase.

If you're selling one item, such as a house, car or business, use the next ritual in the book. This ritual is for people who are selling something on an ongoing basis.

Although much simpler than previous rituals, it is often effective within days, but works more efficiently when you have already completed the Master Money Ritual at least once.

For this ritual, you don't imagine a negative state and then transmute it into a positive one. Instead, you notice the current state of affairs regarding your sales, and then push that feeling back in time, as though it is history, and replace it with a new feeling, as though your sales have increased. By making your current emotions feel like a memory, and by experiencing increased sales in the present moment (using your imagination) you fire up the magick in the talisman.

Before you begin, try to remember how you actually felt about your real sales one month ago. Compare that feeling to your current feeling. It may be that sales have improved or worsened over the month, but that isn't the point. The point is that memories have a slightly different quality to the way they feel. Notice this difference. In the ritual you will change a current emotion to feel like a memory, so become familiar with the qualities and sensations of a memory, so you can replicate that.

Find a few minutes when you are free to work on this ritual in peace, and let your eyes scan all the words in the talisman. Scan from right to left, completing each line and then moving down to the next until you have seen all the letter shapes.

Think about your current sales, but instead of thinking about the sales figures themselves, try to focus on the emotional reaction you have to your current sales. It may be a positive reaction. You may feel good about your current sales, but not quite as excited as you want to be. You may be worried about current sales levels. If so, let yourself experience that fear. Your emotions about your current sales may be subtle or intense, and whatever you feel is right. Don't try to pretend a feeling, but notice how you honestly feel about your current sales.

Although I've said you shouldn't focus on the figures, it may be impossible to generate the required emotions without contemplating those figures. The important point is that you don't stay focused on the figures, but work with the emotions they generate. But you don't have to clear your mind of all numbers, in the fear that it will damage the ritual. If the numbers occur to you, that's fine, but then let them go and work with the feeling they have generated.

Say the following words:

KEY MAL-ACH-AV
YITZ-AV-EH LACH
LISH-MORE-CHAH-BUH-CHOL
DUH-RACH-ECH-AH

You may want to check the pronunciation guide at the back of the book to help with these words. A good vocal flow is more important than an objectively correct pronunciation. These words are represented by a letter acronym within the talisman, which makes it Pronunciation Proof. The words are a simple call that guides the angelic powers to respond to your request.

If you cannot say the words out loud, imagine calling them out, and know that they are being heard by angelic powers.

With a little imagination you can change your feelings to be more like a memory. Change the emotion you are feeling to a memory. Essentially, you pretend that what you're feeling is something that you felt a month ago. By pretending that what you feel is in the past, you make room for a new emotion.

Now allow yourself to feel good about increased sales. (You're now pretending to be one month in the future, but you should feel it as though it's happening right now.)

Once again, you do not worry about the figures, but imagine how good you feel now that your sales have increased by a large amount. Feel the emotion as though this has already happened.

When you get this right, it should feel as though the magick has already worked. You're feeling good about your sales, with the memory of your previous sales now made insignificant by the pleasure you're experiencing.

Begin to scan the words in the sigil once more, from right to left, one line at a time. As you scan each line, let yourself feel grateful for your increased sales and the pleasure they have brought you. You can even think the words 'thank you', as you scan each word.

When you scan the final line, the ritual is over. You can say, 'It is done,' and then close the book to signify that the ritual is complete.

Perform this ritual for three days in a row. Repeat this ritual whenever you want to see an increase in sales. When starting out, some people perform it for three days every month. The results can manifest rapidly, even overnight, or there may be a very gradual change. Performing the ritual every month makes you less likely to lust for short-term results, and can let this magick work over the long-term.

Ensure that you do all you can in the real world to improve your sales, and the magick will always reward your efforts.

The talisman appears on the following page.

כמיל לבד

שדי
מטטרון
יהואל
הימצעצמיה

א ט ד

ת ה ז

ד ה ד

Ritual for Buying and Selling

This ritual works whenever you're selling something, and can even get you the best deal when you are buying. It is aimed at getting the best possible deal when you are selling or buying a house, car, business, or even when you're selling an old guitar.

The ritual itself is extremely simple, and involves looking at the talisman while noticing and transmuting your emotions. You also employ a simple visualization that will be familiar to readers of *Magickal Protection*.

To begin with, think about the object, item or property that you want to buy or sell, and notice your current emotions while gazing at the talisman. Gaze at the whole shape of the talisman. See it as a black diamond. Gaze passively at the black shape. You will notice lines and letters, but you do not need to pay attention to them. Continue to notice how you feel about the potential deal. You may feel fear, anxiety, hope, excitement or dread, or you may even feel that you don't want the deal to go ahead at all. You may feel almost nothing. Whatever you actually feel in the moment, allow yourself to feel it fully and honestly.

Now imagine the pleasure of getting a good deal, while still gazing at the talisman. Turn your attention to the white lines and letters in the talisman. Look at all the lines and letters without staring, but look at them with more focus than before. It doesn't matter in what order you see the various lines and letters, only that you see every letter and shape that is before you. You are not trying to read or understand. This is a way of letting the talisman sink into your consciousness. Do this as you imagine that you have got exactly the deal you want. If you are selling, notice the emotion of getting a fantastic deal. If you're buying, feel as though you've got a bargain. As with all the rituals in this book, you should not think about the actual amount of money that would create this feeling. You only focus on the feeling.

When you can feel the emotion of a good result, which should feel as though it has already come to pass, allow the letters to glow bright white. It is as though diamond starlight is passing through the letters and shapes. Let bright light shine through. There is no need to speak any words. As the light glows through the talisman, change your emotion to one of gratitude. Feel as though the result has already come to pass, and as you see the white light in the talisman, feel grateful that you got exactly what you were hoping for.

This part of the process only needs to last for about a minute, although some people enjoy making it last longer. When it feels right to do so, let the light in the sigil fade. Now create *Light From The Dark*, as instructed earlier, and allow the light to pass into the talisman. The ritual is complete.

Sometimes, during this ritual, you will get a very clear intuition that you no longer want the deal to go ahead. I once used this ritual when buying a house, hoping to get a good deal, but instead I got the very strong feeling that I should not pursue the deal at all. My intuition probably told me that, in those circumstances, it was impossible to get the deal I was looking for, and so it was better to walk away.

This can happen even when you don't get a jolt of intuition. Sometimes, you will perform this ritual and then find that you are unable to buy or sell. This means the most appropriate time has not yet come.

Most often, though, the result is that you get exactly the deal you are looking for, fast. Whether you're selling something to get rid of it, or buying something such as a house, car or business, you will find that you get a good financial deal, and that any contractual details are ironed out with ease.

The ritual only needs to be performed once. If circumstances change – because you decide you want to buy a different house, for example – repeat the ritual. Otherwise, one working is enough.

What if you're buying or selling several things at once? You can use this ritual on several different targets at once, but make sure you leave an hour or so between each ritual, and perform the full ritual for each thing you are trying to buy or sell.

ידהמובה
ד דודניאל
מ משפידאל
ב ביבאל

border (repeating): חשגביבא יה צורבא טובארא

Get Somebody to Pay Up

When somebody owes you money, and is refusing to pay, or delaying payment, you can use magick to get paid. It makes sense to use legally worded letters, and other forms of debt collection where possible, but I hear many stories of loans within families, corrupt business owners and petty criminals who refuse to pay up.

When I first started writing for a living, I found that getting paid was almost as difficult as getting the work in the first place. This magick helped to turn that around. It can be used when people are deliberately withholding money, delaying payment, or just being lazy and inefficient about paying you.

The ritual is similar to the previous working, and involves looking at a talisman while noticing and transmuting your emotions, and performing a simple visualization.

Think about the money that is owed to you, but rather than thinking about the amount, think about the other associations connected to this situation; consider the person, people or the business that owes you money, and think about how they make you feel. Keeping your thoughts off the actual money, let yourself become upset, angry or just impatient with the late payment. You may find that the money intrudes on your thoughts. If somebody owes you $5000, it's difficult to not think of the $5000 when you're letting yourself experience these emotions. It's fine if the numbers occur to you, but your main focus should be on the way the injustice of this late payments feels to you now.

As these feelings become clear, gaze at the whole shape of the talisman. See it as a black diamond. Gaze passively at the black shape. You will notice lines and letters, but you do not need to pay attention to them. Continue to notice how you feel about the unpaid money.

Now imagine that it's a week later, and the debt has been paid. Again, don't focus on the amount that's owed. Just imagine the intense relief, and feeling of victory, now that the debt has been paid. Turn your attention to the white lines and letters in the talisman. Look at all the lines and letters without staring, but look at them with more focus than before. It doesn't matter in what order you see the various lines and letters, only that you see every letter and shape that is before you. You are not trying to read or understand, but letting your eyes pass over the lines and letters as you feel the rush of pleasure at having been paid what you were rightfully owed.

Allow the letters to glow bright white. It is as though diamond starlight is passing through the letters and shapes. Let bright light shine through and change your emotion to one of gratitude. Feel as though the result has already come to pass, and as you see the white light in the talisman, feel grateful that you got paid fully and fairly. Feel grateful that justice has been done.

Allow this part of the ritual to last for about a minute, or longer if you prefer, but for no more than a couple of minutes. Let the light in the sigil fade. Now create *Light From The Dark*, as instructed earlier, and allow the light to pass into the talisman. The ritual is complete.

When it comes to bad debts, it can be quite difficult to let go of your lust for a rapid and fair result. If you find yourself thinking about the debt, remember that you have performed this magick, and remember how grateful you felt at the end of the ritual. Bring that feeling to the forefront of your consciousness, rather than dwelling on the injustice of the debt, or the problems it causes.

The ritual only needs to be performed once. If you get no results at all, you can repeat it after a week, but that is rarely required. In extreme cases, you may want to use this ritual at the same time as the genius ritual to Attract Chance Money, because Nitika is a spirit that is helpful when getting people to pay up.

If several people owe you money, perform a separate ritual on a different day for each person that owes you money. If you are able to use legal services to recover money, do so. Never stop your real world work, because you think the magick will do all the work. Send letters of demand, and make calls, doing all you can to recover the debt. Even if you've tried this approach before, try it again, because now there is magick in place, and your efforts will have additional power.

כהת

אוריאל
בגיאן
הכת

The Genius Rituals

The following chapters explore The Genius Rituals, which employ the powers of intelligent spirits. These spirits are sometimes thought of as personifications of qualities and powers. The spirit Nitika, for example, is known as the genius of precious stones. This does not mean that Nitika actually attracts diamonds, but that the qualities of gems – something rare, beautiful and precious - can be drawn to you.

Knowing how to interpret the qualities of the various genii has taken a great deal of research and experimentation. We have found that by getting the genii to work in harmony with each other, you can create extremely effective money magick.

Every genius ritual contains a talisman for several genii. These talismans contain a central sigil, along with an outer square containing words of power spelt in a celestial alphabet. A version of the genius name is also written in the celestial alphabet. These sigils give you direct contact with the genii, but each genius ritual is overseen, empowered and made safe by the archangel Raziel.

There are many ways to contact Raziel, including chants, ritual calls and words of power. In this context, you will use a sigil of Raziel to establish contact, while speaking ritual words.

Once you have made contact with Raziel you will go on to connect with the genius spirits directly, and ask that they transform your reality to reflect the emotional state that you desire.

Before moving on to the following chapters, become familiar with this method for calling on Raziel.

The following ritual involves the use of divine names, a sigil and a series of calls to ensure that Raziel hears you. The archangel will then guide the genius spirits to hear you and to work in harmony, bringing about the result you desire.

An effective way to contact higher spirits, such as archangels, is to use imaginary lightning while you sing the angel's name. To do this you imagine a bolt of lightning striking you when you sing Raziel's name.

As you call the name, you picture lightning coming down from the clouds, striking you and returning to heaven. Imagine that it forges a connection between yourself and Raziel. (In the real world, lighting strikes the ground and then returns to the sky in an instant, so this is what you should imagine.)

Angels respond to our voices when we sing their names. You don't need to sing well, or even sing a particular tune. You don't need to sing loudly or impressively. All you need to do is make the angelic name sound as though it is being sung. One note will do, although many people find it easy to sing three notes, as Raziel has three syllables.

During this ritual you speak the words, and only the name of Raziel is sung. It is pronounced RAH-ZEE-ELL.

At the beginning of each ritual, spend a few minutes gazing at the sigil of Raziel. Your gaze should not be a focused attempt to read the words or understand what is written there. Rather than scanning individual letters, let your eyes take in the whole sigil at once. It might help if you hold the book further away from you than usual, but not so far away that the details of the sigil become obscure.

Know that contemplating this sigil will stir your spirit to connect with the archangel Raziel. Before you even utter a word, the connection is being made.

Speak these words:

> This is the beginning.
> I open the way.

Reach both arms forward, holding them straight out in front of you, with the backs of the hands touching (thumbs toward the ground). Now move your hands apart, as though your palms are opening the space before you.

Speak these words (singing RAH-ZEE-ELL):

> ACH-AT-REE-ELL
> EE-AH
> EE-AH-OH-EH
> TZ-VAH-OTT
> HAHD-EAR-EAR-ON
> RAH-ZEE-ELL
> RAH-ZEE-ELL
> RAH-ZEE-ELL

Look at the sigil for a few seconds, and know that Raziel hears your call.

Speak these words (singing RAH-ZEE-ELL):

> Oh mighty Raziel (RAH-ZEE-ELL),
> let my voice be heard by
> (*Here, you will name the spirits and their powers*).
> I seal this command with the word of power
> AH-RAH-REE-TAH).

Look at the sigil and feel gratitude for Raziel's presence. You may sense an angelic presence, or you may feel nothing at all. This won't affect your result, so feel gratitude for Raziel's presence, and then continue with the particular genius ritual that you have chosen.

You may find that it helps to write out the instructions above, so that you can place the Raziel sigil in front of you, and read from your notes, rather than having to scan backward and forward through the book as you work. You can do the same for the genius ritual itself, writing out the details that you need, making it easy to look at the genius talismans without having to flick through the book to find the instructions. Although writing out the details can take time, it will help you to become familiar with the process of the ritual. If you have the print version of the book you may prefer to photocopy all the sigils that you're using, so you can have them all in front of you at once.

During each ritual you will be guided to look at the various parts of each talisman. On each talisman there is a square outline of celestial script. You do not need to look at this consciously. The pattern of lines in the upper part of the circle are the sigil of the individual spirit. In this example, only the spirit's sigil is highlighted.

The large letters beneath the sigil are a form of the spirit's name, written from right to left in celestial script. In this example, only the spirit's name is highlighted.

There is no need to study these talismans in detail, but when you come to the specific instructions, it's important to know which part is the sigil and which part is the name.

On the following page you will find the sigil for Raziel, and this is the one you should use in the opening part of the ritual.

The Sigil of Raziel

Attract Money Through Perception

For some people, making money is all about reading markets, predicting trends and knowing what's going to happen next. Whether you work with real estate or the stock market, you need the ability to perceive the future. This ritual is a way of extending your perception, so that you can make accurate and helpful predictions regarding decisions that will affect your income.

If you do not deal with markets of any kind, this ritual can be useful when you want to ensure you get all the facts about a particular situation or deal. If you are considering working with another person or company, finding a new supplier or trying out a new form of advertising, this ritual will help you to know the best course of action. If you're a freelancer, the ritual can help you to discover which markets you can trust, and where it is best to sell your work. For those who work in more regular employment, the ritual can help you to assess job opportunities far more accurately.

For this ritual you need to create the emotion of mystery and transmute it to a sense of knowing. The focus is not on money, but on the pleasure of knowing the information you need to know (which will in turn bring you money).

If you want to work this magick continually, because you work in the markets, for example, you can perform this ritual for three days every month, to enable your perceptions to continually expand. If there is a particular deal or situation that you want to target, you can then run the ritual again at any time, for three days, to discover what you need to know.

If you are more interested in using this as an occasional form of magick, you perform it for three days, targeting it at your specific situation. If, for example, you are a freelance writer, trying to discover which publisher will give you the best deal, you would target the magick directly at that subject.

Find a place where you can be alone, and consider the situation at hand. However, you actually feel about this situation, imagine that the future is cloaked in mystery. Imagine that there are secrets and truths hidden in the future. These truths could bring you great success, but for now they are hidden.

When you can feel the mystery that clouds your situation, contact Raziel. Gaze at the sigil as instructed earlier.

Speak these words:

> This is the beginning.
> I open the way.

Reach both arms forward, holding them straight out in front of you, with the backs of the hands touching (thumbs toward the ground). Now move your hands apart, as though your palms are opening the space before you.

Speak these words (singing RAH-ZEE-ELL):

> ACH-AT-REE-ELL
> EE-AH
> EE-AH-OH-EH
> TZ-VAH-OTT
> HAHD-EAR-EAR-ON
> RAH-ZEE-ELL
> RAH-ZEE-ELL
> RAH-ZEE-ELL

Look at the sigil of Raziel for a few seconds, and know that Raziel hears your call.

Speak these words (singing RAH-ZEE-ELL):

> Oh mighty Raziel (RAH-ZEE-ELL),
> let my voice be heard by
> Sisera (SEES-AIR-AH), genius of desire,
> Labezerin (LAH-BEZ-AIR-IN), genius of success,
> and Eistibus (AY-EE-STI-BUS), genius of divination.
> I seal this command with the word of power
> AH-RAH-REE-TAH).

Look at the sigil of Sisera and then say:

> Sisera (SEES-AIR-AH), genius of desire,
> give me the power to perceive the truth that I crave.

Read the celestial script that spells Sisera's name, from right to left, several times. As you do so, know that through the powers of magickal desire you can know the truth about your situation.

Look at the sigil of Labezerin and then say:

> Labezerin (LAH-BEZ-AIR-IN), genius of success,
> give me the power to discover the path to knowledge.

Read the celestial script that spells Labezerin's name, from right to left, several times. As you do so, know that through the powers of pure success, you have the ability to find the right pathway to discover vital knowledge.

Look at the sigil of Eistibus and then say:

> Eistibus (AY-EE-STI-BUS), genius of divination,
> give me the power to know the future.

Read the celestial script that spells the name of Eistibus, from right to left, several times. As you do so, know that through the powers of divination, you can discover the truth about your situation.

Create *Light From The Dark*, as described earlier, and pour the energy into the sigils of Sisera, Labezerin and Eistibus. You can do this one by one, or if you have printed copies or photocopies, you can arrange all the sigils before you and pour the light into all of them at once. There is no need to empower the Raziel sigil, as it is only used to contact Raziel, and that is achieved easily.

To close the ritual, close the book and sit for a while, feeling grateful that you have the power of perception. Where there was mystery, there is now clarity. Avoid thinking about the money this can bring you, but feel grateful that you can perceive all that you need to perceive about this situation.

In the coming days, you may get flashes of insight, moments of intuition, a sense of knowing, or a growing certainty about the situation you are dealing with. In some cases, you may see truths in your dreams. Trust your intuition, and trust the feelings you have about these flashes of intuition, and they will guide you to success.

Sisera

Labezerin

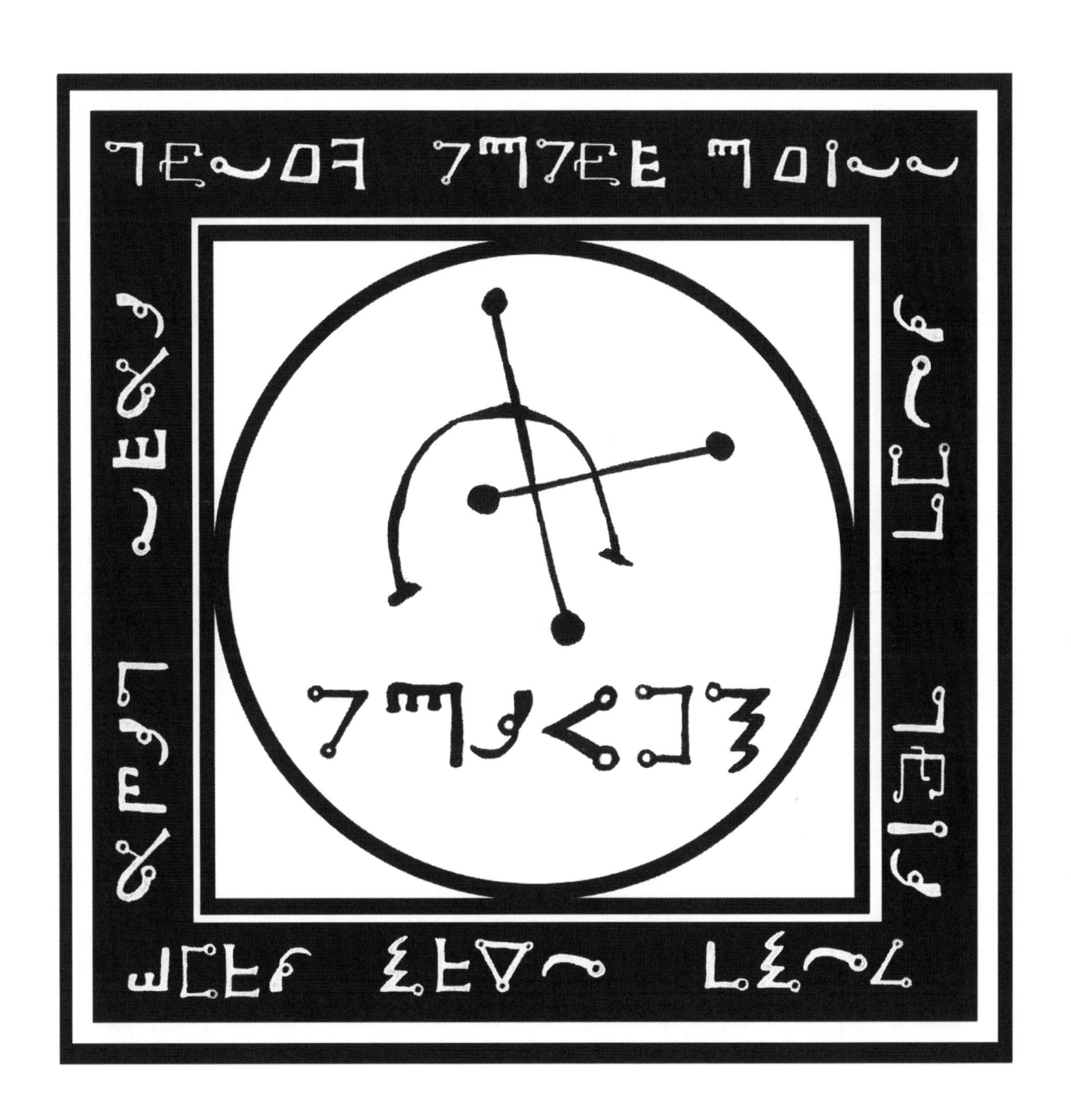

Eistibus

Chance Money Attraction

You can't usually live off money that turns up out of the blue, but that doesn't stop it being an enjoyable way to get a funding boost. *Magickal Cashbook* became popular because it employs the power of the genius spirit Nitika to attract a specific sum of money, which usually arrives in an unexpected way. In this book, Nitika works with other genius spirits to find ways to bring you a continual flow of unexpected money.

Perform this ritual for three days. Ideally, these should be consecutive days, but if that's not possible you should avoid stretching out the ritual for longer than a week.

The effects of this ritual can last for more than a month. The effects are also cumulative, so that the more you practice this ritual, the more likely it is to bring results. It often works immediately, but when you become familiar with these spirits, it works with more speed and fluidity. This doesn't mean you should perform it over and over again, every week, in the hope that you will make it more powerful, but that you can repeat the three-day working every month or so. There is no obligation to perform it that often. If you only perform it twice a year, you will still get the cumulative benefits. For some people, the occasional use of the ritual is a satisfactory way to work.

Spend a few moments thinking about how you feel in this exact moment. Notice that, at this moment in time, there are no surprises. Nothing has been gifted to you, and in this very moment, nothing about your life has changed. Although you are performing magick, there is no increase in your pleasure or the joys that could await you.

When you have that feeling clear, contact Raziel. Gaze at the sigil as instructed earlier.

Speak these words:

> This is the beginning.
> I open the way.

Reach both arms forward, holding them straight out in front of you, with the backs of the hands touching (thumbs toward the ground). Now move your hands apart, as though your palms are opening the space before you.

Speak these words (singing RAH-ZEE-ELL):

> ACH-AT-REE-ELL
> EE-AH
> EE-AH-OH-EH
> TZ-VAH-OTT
> HAHD-EAR-EAR-ON
> RAH-ZEE-ELL
> RAH-ZEE-ELL
> RAH-ZEE-ELL

Look at the sigil of Raziel for a few seconds, and know that Raziel hears your call.

Speak these words (singing RAH-ZEE-ELL):

> Oh mighty Raziel (RAH-ZEE-ELL),
> let my voice be heard by
> Nitika (KNEE-TEA-CAH), genius of precious stones,
> Haatan (HA-AH-TAN), genius of concealed treasures,
> Sialul (SEE-AH-LULL), genius of prosperity,
> and Librabis (LIB-RAH-BISS), genius of hidden gold.
> I seal this command with the word of power
> AH-RAH-REE-TAH).

Look at the sigil of Nitika and then say:

> Nitika (KNEE-TEA-CAH), genius of precious stones,
> give me the power to receive things that I value.

Read the celestial script that spells Nitika's name, from right to left, several times. As you do so, know that Nitika can help you receive the things you value. (These may be experiences, objects or anything else that money can buy, but don't focus on the money.)

Look at the sigil of Haatan and then say:

> Haatan (HA-AH-TAN), genius of concealed treasures,
> give me the power to discover hidden wealth.

Read the celestial script that spells Haatan's name, from right to left, several times. As you do so, know that Haatan can help you discover wealth. (Think of wealth in terms of experience and emotion, rather than hard cash.)

Look at the sigil of Sialul and then say:

> Sialul (SEE-AH-LULL), genius of prosperity,
> give me the power to enjoy abundance.

Read the celestial script that spells Sialul's name, from right to left, several times. As you do so, know that Sialul can bring you an abundance of pleasures.

Look at the sigil of Librabis and then say:

> Librabis (LIB-RAH-BISS), genius of hidden gold,
> give me the power to find hidden riches.

Read the celestial script that spells the name of Librabis, from right to left, several times. As you do so, know that Librabis can surprise you with riches. (Again, think of rich experiences and your pleasure in using and enjoying wealth, rather than in the money itself.)

Create *Light From The Dark*, as described earlier, and pour the energy into the sigils of Nitika, Haatan, Sialul and Librabis. You can do this one by one, or if you have printed copies or photocopies, you can arrange all the sigils before you and pour the light into all of them at once. There is no need to empower the Raziel sigil.

To close the ritual, close the book and sit for a while, feeling grateful that you can attract abundance from out of the blue, and that a wealth of pleasure will come to you from unexpected places. Notice that the earlier feeling of stasis that you created at the beginning of the ritual, is gone, and feel grateful that you are now in a state of flow, where surprises, gifts and unexpected pleasures come into your life continually. Feel the gratitude as though the result has already happened, and then get on with your day, without looking or waiting for a result.

You can find the sigil of Raziel earlier in the book. The sigils of the genius spirits you need for this ritual appear on the following pages.

Nitika

Haatan

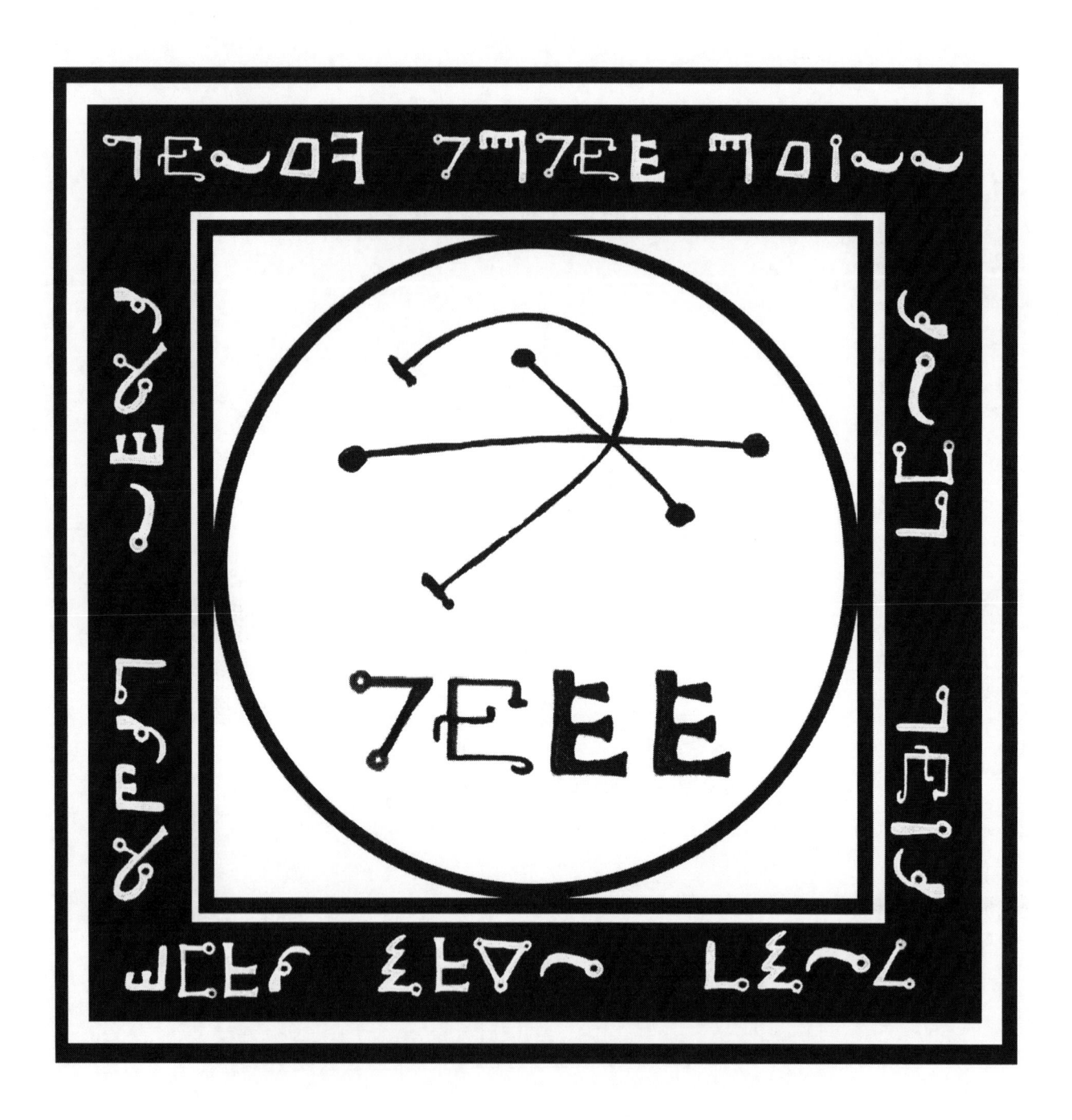

Sialul

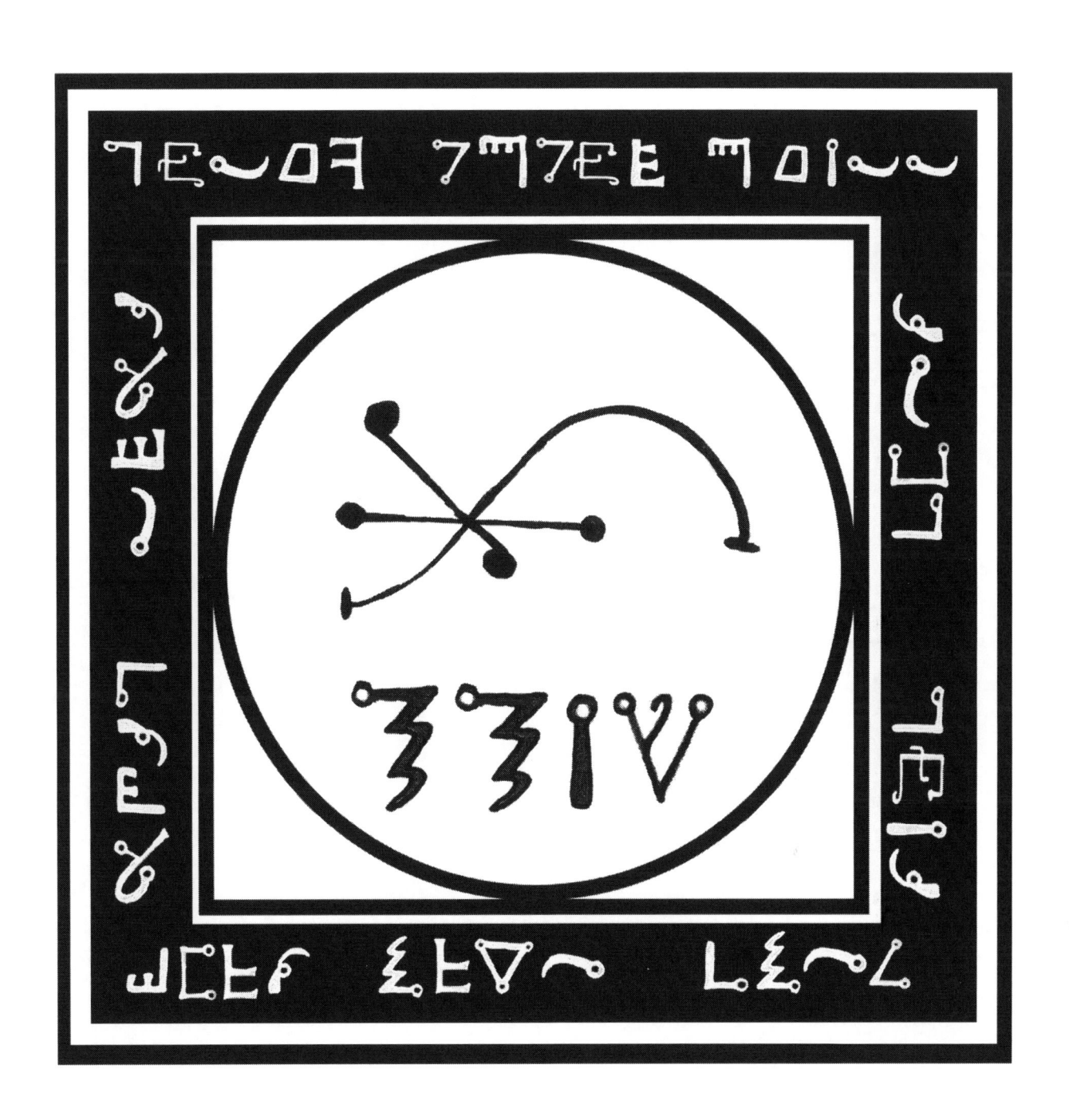

Librabis

The Gambling Ritual

In *Magickal Cashbook* I said that, 'When you give up gambling, you're sending a message out to the universe that you trust that money will turn up. That is way more powerful than hoping for a win.'

I also pointed out that magick doesn't tend to work for lotteries, because you are trying to change a phenomenally random event. There are many things that magick can control, but the more variables that come into play, the more difficult it is for magick to have an effect. Randomly bouncing balls are far more difficult to control than, say, your boss, who could give you a raise or promotion. This is why most of the magick we share is based around methods that do not involve gambling.

Why, then, am I including a gambling ritual in this book? Firstly, there is great demand for this magick, because lots of people enjoy casual gambling, and they want to find an extra edge. Secondly, although you can't change the way the numbers fall, you can use magick to divine what the numbers may be. That can work. Thirdly, there are other forms of gambling, such as playing poker, that involve a degree of skill. Magick can certainly help in these cases.

This ritual is the last one in the book because I know it is the first one that you may be tempted to use. If you work in a stable job, with little chance of promotion, you may see no other way that money could come to you. I urge you to think again, and know that money can come in so many creative ways, that you should see gambling as an entertaining sideline, rather than as a reliable way of making money.

This gambling ritual has brought wonderful results for many, but do not expect huge wins, and do not expect to win all the time. If you're a regular gambler, your winnings should improve. If you gamble occasionally, for fun, you should get some pleasant surprises. If you play a game that involves your own skill, rather than pure chance, you should see a great improvement in your winnings.

There are several important factors that need to be addressed for this magick to work. You must not perform this ritual as a last, desperate hope when you have no money left and *need* a good result. You should only use this ritual when things are going quite well and you can spare the money. You should only gamble when it feels ok to lose the money. If you're going to feel bad about losing the money, don't gamble.

You need to enjoy playing the game, whether you win or not. That is, you need to derive pleasure from the act of playing, and the fun of taking part, whether it is a game of skill or chance, rather than merely praying for a jackpot. If you can find a way to make this a pleasant activity, and one that you *don't* rely on for income, the magick will work.

If you're not going to win, where's the fun? People gamble for many reasons. Some play due to an addiction, and some because they enjoy the challenge of the game. Others play because they know they have just as much chance of winning the lottery as anybody else, which makes it a more level playing field than the ordinary world. And some play because there is a real thrill in knowing that the moment you roll the dice, so to speak, anything could happen. You buy a lottery ticket, and it makes you giggle to think that you could be a millionaire by morning. Finding pleasure in the act of playing the game is essential, so do not gamble with magick if you are feeling extremely poor or unwilling to lose. The happier you are to lose, the more likely you are to win.

If you use this ritual for a month and then say, 'I played the lottery every week and won nothing,' I won't be all that surprised. The odds are so far against you winning anything at all that it can take time for this magick to break through. The magick will definitely push the odds in your favor, but you are dealing with such remote odds that even a massive improvement in your luck still means that you only have a small chance of winning. Think of it as a fun, long-term project that you're willing to do for the sheer thrill of the game. For serious gamblers who play poker, or gamble with another game of skill, you'll see results more rapidly.

Despite this disclaimer, many people find that this magick works first time.

If you plan on playing the lottery, perform this ritual for three consecutive days (no more than a week before the draw), focusing on the specific lottery that you want to enter. If you are entering several lotteries, consider them all during the ritual. On the fourth day, choose the numbers that you want to play. Use any method you like to choose the numbers. You can ponder the list of numbers, draw numbers out of a bag, or think of numbers randomly. Whatever you do, don't stick with an old set of numbers. As mentioned, your magick won't change the way the balls fall, so it won't make your old numbers any better. The best it can do is give you a chance of discovering numbers that will be useful in the future.

If you are using another form of gambling, such as visiting a casino to play roulette, again perform the ritual for three days, with the game occurring some time during the four days that follow the completion of the ritual. So, if you plan on playing poker on Saturday night, you could perform the ritual on Wednesday, Thursday and Friday, ready for your game on Saturday. Or you could perform it on Monday, Tuesday and Wednesday, ready for a Sunday game.

What if you can't perform the ritual on consecutive days? If you have to skip a day or two, that's fine, but don't spread this working out for more than a week. Get the three rituals performed within a single week. If you're playing the lottery, choose your numbers the day after you complete the ritual. If it's another form of gambling, play the game within four days of completing the ritual.

You only need to perform the ritual for three days the *first* time you use it for a specific outcome. If, for example, you want to play the lottery every week, then you would perform the ritual for three days, play the lottery, and then the next time you play, you only need to perform the ritual for one day. Many people perform the ritual once a week, the day before they pick their numbers.

If you switch to a different game, or even a different lottery, you should perform the ritual for three days in a row the first time you play, and then perform it just once each time you play, a few days before you play.

The effects of the workings can be cumulative, so if you go one week without winnings, never say to yourself, 'It didn't work this week.' Instead, know that the odds may be gradually stacking up in your favor.

When you get a win, no matter how small, enjoy it and relish it and know that chance is shifting to make things better for you.

Find a time and place where you can be alone and undisturbed. Spend a few moments thinking about the game of chance you are going to gamble in, whether it's a lottery or a game involving skill. Know that you have as much chance of losing as you do of winning.

This is not necessarily the objective truth. In a lottery, you have almost no chance of winning, statistically. In a small poker game you might have a one in five chance of winning. That is not the point. This is a small trick that you are playing with your mind and your emotions. Later, you will reverse this perception, ever so slightly, and that is where the power comes in. For now, as you consider the game that lies ahead, imagine that you have the same chance of losing that you have of winning. When you have that feeling clear, contact Raziel. Gaze at the sigil as instructed earlier.

Speak these words:

> This is the beginning.
> I open the way.

Reach both arms forward, holding them straight out in front of you, with the backs of the hands touching (thumbs toward the ground). Now move your hands apart, as though your palms are opening the space before you.

Speak these words (singing RAH-ZEE-ELL):

> ACH-AT-REE-ELL
> EE-AH
> EE-AH-OH-EH
> TZ-VAH-OTT
> HAHD-EAR-EAR-ON
> RAH-ZEE-ELL
> RAH-ZEE-ELL
> RAH-ZEE-ELL

Look at the sigil of Raziel for a few seconds, and know that Raziel hears your call.

Speak these words (singing RAH-ZEE-ELL):

> Oh mighty Raziel (RAH-ZEE-ELL),

let my voice be heard by
Aeglun (EYE-GLUN), genius of lightning,
Butatar (BUT-AT-ARE), genius of calculations,
Aclahayr (AK-LA-HAYER), genius of gambling,
Toglas (TOG-LASS), genius of treasures.
I seal this command with the word of power
AH-RAH-REE-TAH).

Look at the sigil of Aeglun and then say:

Aeglun (EYE-GLUN), genius of lightning,
give me the power to express my will through magick.

Read the celestial script that spells Aeglun's name, from right to left, several times. As you do so, know that through the powers of magick you have as much chance of winning as you do of losing.

Look at the sigil of Butatar and then say:

Butatar (BUT-AT-ARE), genius of calculations,
give me the power to understand numbers.

Read the celestial script that spells Butatar's name, from right to left, several times. As you do so, know that through the power of numbers, you have as much chance of winning as you do of losing. (This may mean choosing numbers, cards, or making other number calculations relevant to your game.)

Look at the sigil of Aclahayr and then say:

Aclahayr (AK-LA-HAYER), genius of gambling,
give me the power to win games of chance.

Read the celestial script that spells Aclahayr's name, from right to left, several times. As you do so, know that through the powers of pure luck you have as much chance of winning as you do of losing.

Look at the sigil of Toglas and then say:

> Toglas (TOG-LASS), genius of treasures,
> give me the power to find glorious wealth.

Read the celestial script that spells Toglas' name, from right to left, several times. As you do so, know that because treasure can be found by anybody, you have as much chance of winning as you do of losing.

Create *Light From The Dark*, as described earlier, and pour the energy into the sigils of Aeglun, Butatar, Aclahayr and Toglas. You can do this one by one, or if you have printed copies or photocopies, you can arrange all the sigils before you and pour the light into all of them at once. There is no need to empower the Raziel sigil.

To close the ritual, close the book and sit for a while, feeling grateful that you have as much chance of winning as you do of losing. Note that you should not feel grateful for a win. You should not picture yourself winning and feeling great about the result. Instead, feel grateful that this magick has given you an *even* chance of winning. And then play your game, making sure you enjoy yourself.

The sigil of Raziel appears earlier in the book, while the sigils of the genius spirits required for this ritual appear on the following pages.

Aeglun

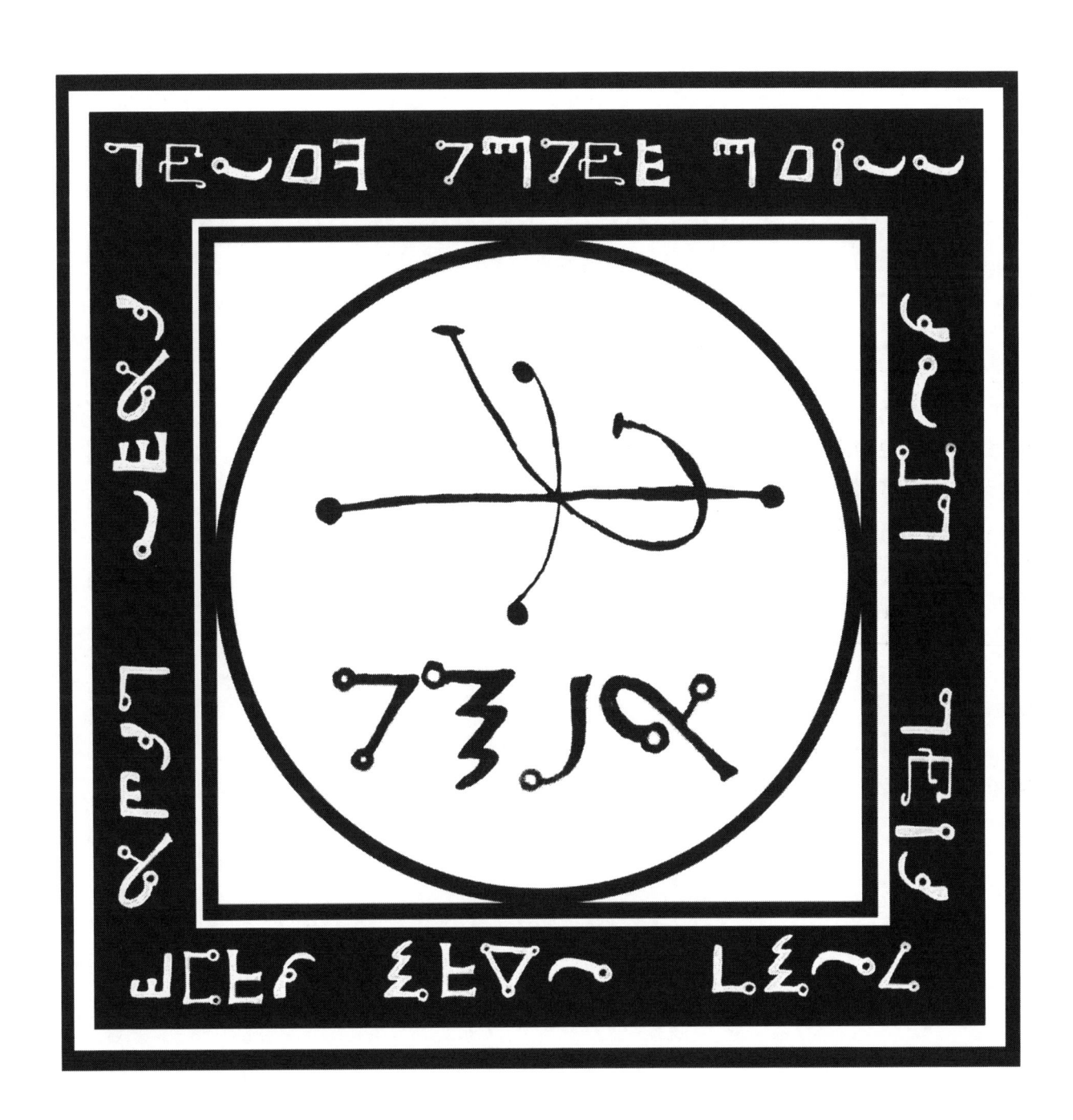

Butatar

Aclahayr

Toglas

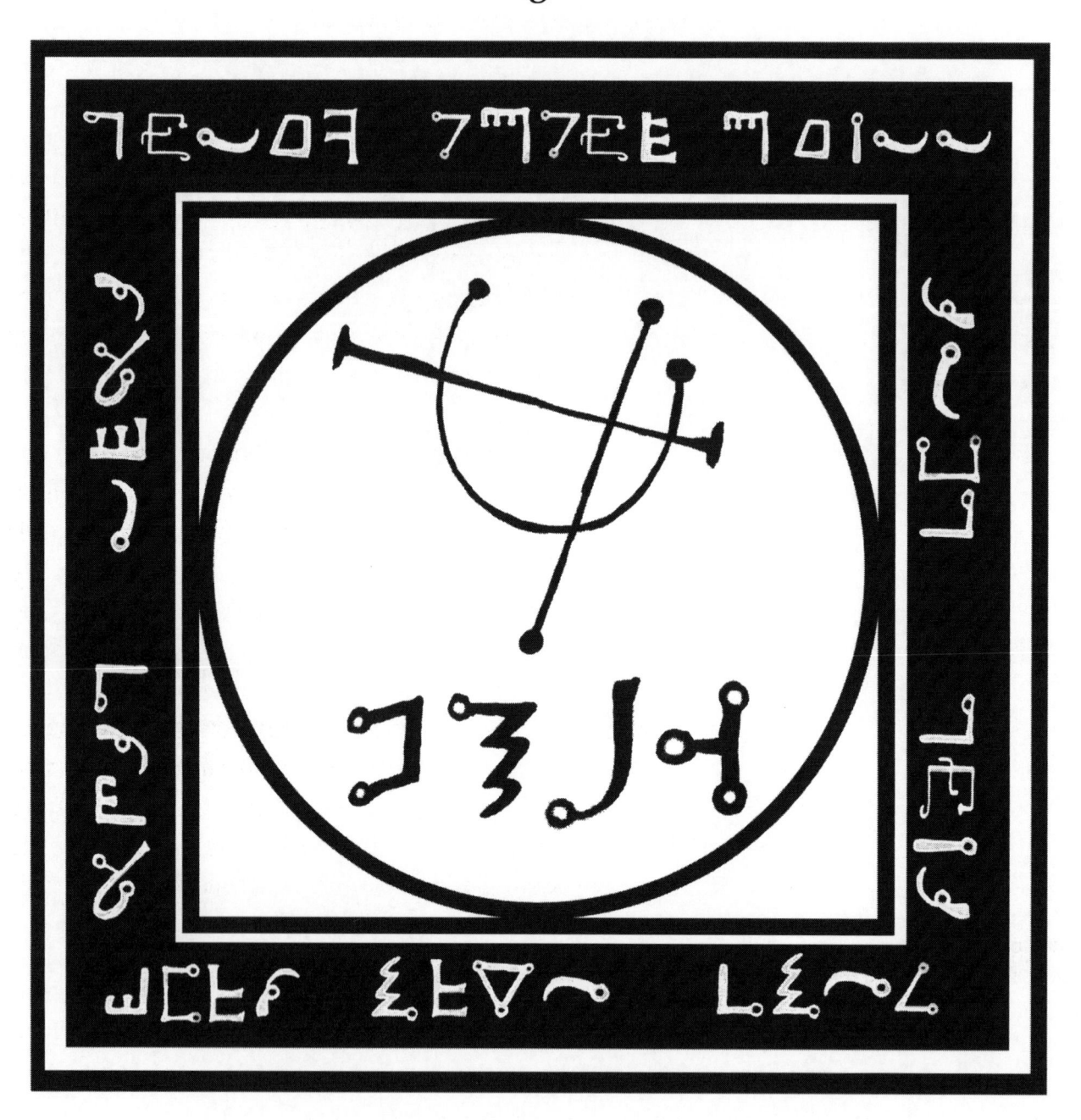

Unleashing the Flow of Money

Some people use money magick and start receiving money within hours or days. Others notice that the magick is working, but find it difficult to manifest as much money as they want. This is often due to deep-seated feelings about money that are often quite sensible and reasonable.

Despite being reasonable and logical, these feelings can slow the flow of money. This chapter contains ideas and techniques that can get money magick working, whatever problems you may have had with money in the past.

I have often said that I don't really like tithing. Some people swear by the principal of tithing, where you give away ten percent of your income to a church or to people in need. While there is nothing wrong with that (and it can make you more relaxed about letting go of money), I find it relatively ineffective because it is too automatic. It feels like an obligatory tax rather than a pleasant donation, and therefore doesn't have the potency of deliberate giving.

If, however, you find yourself feeling bad about the thought of being rich, simply know that you can and will gain pleasure from sharing your money. You can share it with friends and family as well as the poor and needy. There is great pleasure to be had in sharing money, so it can be useful to imagine this pleasure alongside the other pleasures of money. Simply picturing this can help to ease any hang-ups you may have about wealth.

If you get what you genuinely want from life, you are more use to others and to the world, than when you are struggling in poverty. There is nothing spiritual about earning money the hard way. There is nothing spiritual about resentment. And there is nothing inherently spiritual about being poor. Suffering is suffering, and it's better to be shut of it.

The only way to make money is to get it to flow from somewhere else, to you, and then let it flow out again as you spend it. If you feel resentful of anybody who makes money, you will tighten up the flow of money.

This problem is solved, in part, by focusing on the emotional results you want, rather than a sum of money. That has been the entire focus of this book, but there is also something you can do to clear your attitude to receiving money.

There are many long-winded ways you can go about erasing negative attitudes to money, but the simplest way is to start living as though money isn't an issue. I am not suggesting that you start spending crazily, or acting like you think the rich would act, but that you find a way to be extremely casual about money. To do this, you can try a bit of traditional folk magick.

I am not a fan of most folk magick. Often it involves nothing more than superstition and small symbolic acts that lack the frisson of real magick. Sometimes, though, I've come across folk magick that is as potent as the highest ceremonial magick.

What follows is not original. Everything else that preceded this chapter is unique to this book, and previously unpublished, but I cannot take credit for this folk magick. You can read about it in many other books. I was told about it many decades ago, by a woman in my village who was thought of as the local witch, and I assumed she'd invented it, but I've since found it all over the place. It's covered in many other books and is included here only because for others, and myself, it did more to unlock the flow of money than anything else. Once the locks were removed, the rest of the magick began to work extremely well. My mistake was that I didn't use it straight away. I waited many years before giving this a try. I urge you to try it out much sooner.

This folk magick involves giving away a small amount of money. I am not talking about tithing or giving to charity. Instead, this magick requires you to leave money where somebody else will find it. You leave it, and you don't look back, but you enjoy knowing that somebody else is going to get pleasure from your small gift. As simple as it sounds, this is extremely powerful.

You shouldn't give away too much, because it might leave you feeling guilty or poor, but you shouldn't give so little that it feels pointless. You want to leave enough money so that when somebody finds it, that money will feel like a pleasant gift. In most cases, $5 will do fine. Although $5 is nothing to many people, and a small fortune to the very poor, you can safely assume that just about anybody who finds $5 will be slightly thrilled.

If giving away $5 is going to make you unhappy, try $1 to begin with.

Alternatively, if you were planning to spend $20 on the lottery this week, you could give away one gift of $10 and two gifts of $5. Do whatever feels enjoyable to you. Never do this if it stops being fun.

It's vital that the recipient of your gift knows that this is a gift, rather than something that was lost. This is why you should attach a small note that says something along the lines of, 'Here is a gift of money for you to enjoy.' I often use a Post-it note to stick the money to a suitable wall – the note glues the money in place, while also delivering the message.

It is essential that you leave the gift and do not wait to see who receives it. Although you might be tempted to watch somebody find the gift, don't wait around. You are meant to be letting go of money, joyfully, so take pleasure in creating a secret moment of surprise. Put the money in place and go.

You really can leave the money just about anywhere, but make sure you aren't seen leaving it, and make sure you will be away from it when it's found. Keep this magick secret. Do not tell others about the small gifts you are leaving, as that tends to weaken the energy of the working. Keeping the secret adds to the pleasure.

Why does giving away a small amount of money do any good at all? Firstly, it's great fun, picturing the surprise and pleasure that a complete stranger will get from finding this money.

Secondly, you have not only shared money, but you have shared the idea of enjoying money. Your note tells the recipient to enjoy the money, so in all likelihood they will treat themselves to a small pleasure, rather than just putting the money away with the rest of their cash. Some people will give it to charity, while others will buy cigarettes. It doesn't matter. Money has begun to flow through you in a pleasant way.

Finally, by enjoying the act of 'spending' or releasing money, you are performing one of the most important magickal acts. Resentful spending makes money dry up. Joyous spending makes it flow. This folk magick works because it loosens up your feelings about money.

If you try this and don't enjoy it, then stop. If it feels like fun, do it every now and then. It's not something you have to do daily, although there have been times when I did this every day for a week or so, to ensure that I really enjoyed letting go of money.

You can do this once a year or once a month. So long as it feels like an enjoyable game, rather than an obligation, it is worth doing every so often. If you find that you're feeling stuck with money, or if you get a particularly large bill, that's the perfect time to try this magick, to loosen things up. The sooner you can enjoy letting go of money, the sooner more will come to you.

Many people say that within three days you will see the amount you gave away returned to you ten-fold or a hundred fold. Some even suggest that you should 'ask the universe', by saying something like, 'Thank you for the $500 you will provide in return for this gift'.

You are free to try this, but I don't think that approach is required, and it may actually hinder the flow, because it makes you fixate on a number and a result, and then three days later you might go, 'Hang on, where's my $500?' I believe that it's better to know that letting go of money joyously attracts more. Enjoy the moment of letting go, and enjoy knowing that more money will come to you continually, but don't put a figure or time limit on this magick.

Getting Money to Flow

If you want this magick to work, there is a catch. You must read the book fully and you should practice the rituals as described. By the time you get here, you may have skipped bits, and jumped straight in. To do so is to risk failure. The information in the early chapters is as important as the ritual descriptions, so make sure you read all the information. I've kept everything as short as possible to make this easy for you. Although it is fine to skip the section on creating *Light From The Dark* until later, you should read everything else to ensure success.

I have published several successful magick books, and most people get great results with them, but I have found that one of the major stumbling blocks to effective magick is that many people only skim-read the books, rather than taking in all the information with real focus. Skim reading is great for getting an overview of what's on offer, but then it's vital that you read all the instructions.

There are some readers who skip straight to the rituals, assuming that what comes before isn't as important. This may be due to eager enthusiasm, laziness, arrogance, or impatience, but whatever the reason, it is perfectly understandable. You want results, and you want them fast.

I have rushed into magick more times than I can remember, and I learned that magick should not be rushed. Although this magick can work extremely fast, you should make sure you have read the first part of the book thoroughly before embarking on a ritual. For each ritual, become familiar with the details before diving into the magick.

On the other hand, I don't believe in over-preparation. Too much planning is a waste of time, and it's better to do a lot of easy-going magick than to spend weeks planning a perfect ritual. Once you've read the instructions, you can get on with the rituals and experience the magick

This book is not filled with unnecessary theory. I only put in what you need to know, with short examples that help illustrate a point. My aim is for this book to be completely practical. Where there is repetition it is there to ensure you don't miss the important points. Please make sure that you take everything in and perform the workings as instructed. If you do so, you will get what you are looking for.

When the Magick Works

Please Like the Facebook page for tips and ideas.

https://www.facebook.com/galleryofmagick

The Gallery of Magick blog contains advice, updated on a regular basis. There are many articles on the site that can help to get your magick working.

www.galleryofmagick.com

You can read countless success stories here:

http://galleryofmagick.com/magickal-success-stories/

Damon Brand

Appendix

Pronunciation Guide

The only sound that presents a challenge is CH, as in the name Achatriel (ACH-AT-REE-ELL). The CH is not the sound you find in *choose* or *cheese*. If you know the Scottish word *Loch*, or the German word *Achtung*, that's the CH sound you're aiming for.

Search YouTube or similar sites for the pronunciation of these words (preferably by Scottish and German speakers respectively), and you'll know how to get it right.

If you simply can't get that CH to sound right (and that does happen with some people due to their accent and dialect), then simply use the K sound when you see CH. So for ACH-AT-REE-ELL, you would say AK-AT-REE-ELL. This is not ideal, but it will still work.

Note that the AH sound is used quite often. This is the English word *ah*, which rhymes with *ma* and *pa*.

Pronunciation does not have to be accurate. It is better to be relaxed about the sounds than to aim for perfection.

EE-AH

EE is like *bee* without the *b*. AH is like the English word *ah*.

TZ-VAH-OTT

TZ is like the final part of *rats*. VAH is like *car*, but with a softer ending, sounding more like *cah* than *car*. OTT is the *blot* without the *bl*.

ACH-AT-REE-ELL

ACH uses the CH sound described above. AT is the English word *at*. REE is like *bee*, but with an *r* instead of a *b*. ELL is like *bell* without the *b*.

YOT-ZAF-CHEE-RON

YOT is like *dot* with a *y* instead of a *d*. ZAF is like *gaff*, with a *z* instead of a *g*. CHEE uses the CH sound described above, followed by EE. RON sounds like *gone*, but with a *r* sound rather than a *g*.

MET-A-TRON

This name sounds exactly as written. Metatron.

KEY MAL-ACH-AV

KEY is the English word *key*. MAL is like *pal* with an *m* instead of a *p*. ACH is *a* followed by the CH sound. AV is like the end of *have*.

YITZ-AV-EH LACH

YITS is like *bits*, but with a *y* instead of a *b*, and the *s* is extended into a slight *z* sound. AV is like the end of *have*. EH is like the English word *eh* (the slang for pardon). LACH sounds similar to *lack*, but with the *ck* sound being replaced by the CH sound.

LISH-MORE-CHAH-BUH-CHOL

LISH is like *dish* with an *l* instead of a *d*. MORE is the English word *more*. CHAH sounds like (and rhymes with) *car*, but starts with the CH sound, and ends with a softer sound than an *r*, more like the word *ah*. BUH is like the very first part of *burn*, before you get to the *r* sound. CHOL begins with the CH sound, and rhymes with *doll*.

DUH-RACH-ECH-AH

DUH is a short *d* sound, as in *dark* without the *ark*. RACH is like *rat* without the *t*, followed by the CH sound. ECH is the CH sound, with *eh* in front of it. Ah is like the English *ah*.

RAH-ZEE-ELL

RAH is like *pa*, with and *r* instead of a *p*. ZEE is like *see* with a *z* instead of an *s*. ELL is like *bell* without the *b*.

EE-AH-OH-EH

EE is like *see* without the *s*. AH is the English word *ah*. OH is the English word *oh*. ELL is like bell without the *b*.

HAHD-EAR-EAR-ON

HAHD, like the English word *ah*, with *h* art the front and *d* at the end. EAR and ON are the English words *ear* and *on*.

AH-RAH-REE-TAH

AH is the English word *ah*. RAH is *ah* with *r* at the front. REE is like *see* with *r* instead of an *s*. TAH is *ah* with *t* at the front.

SISERA

108

(SEES-AIR-AH)

SEES is like *seas*, AIR is *air*, and ah is like *ah*.

LABEZERIN
(LAH-BEZ-AIR-IN)

LAH is like the *pa* with an *l* instead of a *p*. BEZ is like the first part of *res*olve, but with a *b* instead of an *r*. AIR is *air*, and IN is *in*.

EISTIBUS
(AY-EE-STI-BUS)

AY is like *pay* without the *p*. EE is like *bee* without the *b*. STI is like *stick* without the *ck*. Bus is the English *bus*.

NITIKA
(KNEE-TEA-CAH)

KNEE is the English word *knee*, and TEA is the word *tea*. CAH sounds like *blah*, but with *c* instead of *bl*.

HAATAN
(HA-AH-TAN)

This words is made from the English words *ha*, *ah* and *tan*.

SIALUL
(SEE-AH-LULL)

This word is made from the English words *see, ah* and *lull*.

LIBRABIS
(LIB-RAH-BISS)

LIB is like *lip*, with a *b* instead of a *p*. RAH is like *pa*, with and *r* instead of a *p*. BISS is like *kiss* with a *b* instead of a *k*.

AEGLUN
(EYE-GLUN)

EYE is the English word *eye*, and GLUN is like *glut* with an *n* instead of a *t*.

BUTATAR
(BUT-AT-ARE)

This word is made from the English words *but, at* and *are*.

ACLAHAYR
(AK-LA-HAYER)

AK is like *back* without the *b*. LA is like *lap* without the *p*. HAYER is like *payer* with an *h* instead of a *p*.

TOGLAS
(TOG-LASS)

TOG is like *fog* with a *t* instead of an *f*. LASS is like *lasso* without the *o*.

Words of Power

'This magic works. Nothing more to say.'

'This wonderful book contains 25 specific magickal actions in a simple, easy-to-read format. The magick in this book works! I use it on a daily basis. It's easy and fast to perform a magick action.'

'I've received immediate results by using the methods as described in this book. You can do these rituals immediately and receive quick results. Words of Power will help you to be the person who you really want to be, help you to have talents and abilities that you've always wanted to, and take your life in the direction that you want it to go.'

'The Words of Power helped heal my relationship with my son and that to me is worth its weight in Gold. Thank you for making this book available.'

Magickal Protection

'This saved my son's life. Only just got this book today and I performed the rituals and two hours later my son survived an attempted robbery at gunpoint. Not a hair on him was harmed. I own all the other books and the magick really works fast. I am so grateful for this.'

'Adding The Sword Banishing and Master Protection Ritual has made all the difference in my workings. Things are coming together much faster and it is more enjoyable.'

'Saved me from a bad car crash. There is no doubt about it, the Angels from the rituals in this jewel of a book will protect you physically. You may not realize how extremely valuable that is until you are in serious jeopardy and wish that someone would come through to help you. If you are on the fence about buying this book, do yourself a GREAT FAVOR and JUST BUY IT. Do the Sword Ritual & Master Ritual and get the attention of these Holy Angels, because believe me when I say that you want them there for you during your time of need. The Master Ritual also has brought the requested peace and harmony into my life.'

Magickal Cashbook

'Enjoy Magick. It Really Works.'

'I've been using Magickal Cashbook for about one month. It has produced immediate and consistent results. The magick in this little book works very well and very fast! If you need quick bursts of cash, this book will absolutely work for you! I'm a singer/songwriter who plays for tips, and the magick in this wonderful book has opened up a nice, steady stream of dollars. Very nice indeed!'

'Give it a chance. This works!'

'Thanks for changing my life.'

'I love this book, the author gets straight to the point, it's easy to understand so it is great for the novice. I've had great results so far, I would recommend this book to anyone looking to increase their cash flow.'

'A little jewel of a book! Easy to read and above all, easy to implement.'

The Magickal Job Seeker

'It works. More than one job offer and out of nowhere, kind of like magick. Yes I got the job!'

'You only need this book, only that!!! With this book I believe that a new golden dawn of magick will follow!!!'

'I have been involved for over 40 years, and I have not had anything work as quickly as what he advises.'

'The people who interviewed me loved me and I didn't have to go through the final rounds of interviews, they just offered me the job. The books written by this author have changed my life and I am deeply grateful. Thank you Damon Brand.'

Damon Brand

www.galleryofmagick.com

Printed in Great Britain
by Amazon